REF
LB 2322 .K3

Kapur, Jagat Narain, 1923-

Current issues in world higher education

REFERENCE

DATE		

FORM 125 M

cop. 1 SOCIAL SCIENCES AND HISTORY DIVISION

The Chicago Public Library

Received OCT 12 1978

© THE BAKER & TAYLOR CO.

CURRENT ISSUES
IN
WORLD HIGHER EDUCATION

CURRENT ISSUES IN WORLD HIGHER EDUCATION

J. N. KAPUR
Ph.D.; F.N.A.Sc.; F.A.Sc.; F.I.M.A.; F.N.A.
Indian Institute of Technology, Kanpur
Ex-Vice-Chancellor, Meerut University.

S.Chand & Company Ltd
RAM NAGAR, NEW DELHI-110055

S. CHAND & COMPANY LTD

Head Office : Ram Nagar, New Delhi-110055
Show Room : 4/16-B, Asaf Ali Road, New Delhi-110002

Branches :

Mai Hiran Gate, Jullundur-144001	285/J, Bipin Behari Ganguli Street
Aminabad Park, Lucknow-226001	Calcutta-700012
Blackie House,	35, Mount Road, Madras-600002
103/5 Walchand Hirachand Marg,	3, Gandhi Sagar East,
Bombay-400001	Nagpur-440002
Khazanchi Road, Patna-800004	K.P.C.C. Building
Sultan Bazar, Hyderabad-500001	Race Course Road, Bangalore-560009

First published 1977

Price : **Rs. 35.00**

*Published by S. Chand & Company Ltd., Ram Nagar, New Delhi-110055
and printed at Rajendra Ravindra Printers (Pvt) Ltd., Ram Nagar,
New Delhi-110055*

PREFACE

The present book and its companion volume "Current Issues in Higher Education in India" reflect the author's experiences of forty-three months of vice-chancellorship of a new and growing university, of attending a couple of international conferences on higher education, of visits to USA, Canada, West Germany, UK, Netherlands, Italy, Australia, Thailand, Singapore and Bangla Desh for studying the systems of higher education there and of attending a dozen national conferences and seminars on various aspects of higher education.

At the International Conference on Implications of Mass Higher Education held at the University of Lancaster in September 1972, I had the unique opportunity of not only listening to delegates from USA, UK, Canada, France, Belgium, Spain, West Germany, Japan and other developed countries describing the implications of mass higher education for their own countries, but I had also the opportunity to discuss personally with delegates from both developing and developed countries many problems of higher education in the background of my knowledge of the higher education situation in India. The first thirteen chapters (except the eleventh) are essentially based on the discussions there and subsequent correspondence with some educationists abroad. The eleventh chapter on mass higher education in China is based on some first-hand accounts given by some visitors to China after the Cultural Revolution there.

The next five chapters are based on my close study of the higher education and research systems in Australia made during a five-week visit to that country at the invitation of the Australian Vice-Chancellors' committee. I had detailed discussions with about one hundred educationists whom I met during my visit to eleven of the fifteen universities in Australia.

I gave fifteen seminars and a number of popular lectures during this visit and very interesting and useful discussions took place after the seminars and lectures.

The next two chapters are based on my visit to West Germany which I visited (as member of a four-man delegation of Indian vice-chancellors) at the invitation of the German Foreign Office. We visited nine universities, six scientific establishments and twelve educational, cultural and scientific organisations.

The last-but-one chapter is based on a seminar on comparative study of Indian and American systems of higher education organised by the US Educational Foundation of India sometime back. This also reflects my personal experiences of visits to about sixty American and Canadian universities in 1969-70.

All these chapters give one a feeling of great turmoil in higher education thinking all over the world. Revolutionary innovations are being suggested and even tried out in many countries of the world. Some of these are discussed in the final chapter. Throughout the book, comparisons are made with the Indian system of higher education. Chapters 13, 18, 20, 21 specially highlight this study in comparative education.

There is a great demand for restructuring of our system of higher education in India. There is a similar demand in almost all countries of the world. We look for models elsewhere in order to develop our own models suited to our genius and needs. This model is also not going to be static but has to be dynamic to meet changing social, economic and political situations. Comparative Education should be a serious subject of study in our universities.

It is hoped that this book will provoke serious thinking and debate and lead to increased interest in Comparative Education in our country.

J. N. KAPUR

CONTENTS

1. Implications of mass higher education ... 1
2. Structures in mass higher education ... 4
3. Continuing mass higher education ... 13
4. Students in mass higher education ... 20
5. Mass higher education in USA ... 25
6. Mass higher education in UK ... 29
7. Mass higher education in Western Europe ... 34
8. Mass higher education in Eastern Europe ... 39
9. Mass higher education in Canada ... 41
10. Mass higher education in Japan ... 46
11. Mass higher education in China ... 4
12. The Open University of UK ... 5
13. Implications for India of mass higher education ... 4
14. Education and research activities in Adelaide ... 65
15. Education and research activities in Canberra ... 72
16. Education and research activities in Melbourne ... 93
17. Education and research activities in Sydney, Newcastle, Townsville and Brisbane ... 101
18. A comparative study of Indian and Australian systems of education ... 105
19. Higher education and research in West Germany ... 123
20. A comparative study of Indian and West German Systems of education ... 133
21. A comparative study of Indian and American systems of education ... 143
22. Innovations in Higher education in various countries of the world ... 159

I

IMPLICATIONS OF MASS HIGHER EDUCATION

1. Interest in higher education has greatly increased all around the world during the last 25 years. Developing countries see in higher education the most important means of scientific, technological and industrial progress, so vital for them for the removal of poverty and for developing affluent societies. Higher education is also the means for them of modernising their societies and for producing highly educated leaders in all walks of life, who will be imbued with their highest ethical and moral ideals. Developed post-industrial societies find themselves moving rapidly from the elitistic system of higher education of the past to the mass higher education of the immediate future and to the universal higher education of a more distant future.

2. This transition to mass higher education has many implications for these societies. As such an international conference was held at Lancaster University, England, to discuss these implications in all their ramifications. Delegates from about 40 countries attended this conference.

3. The conference concentrated on the study of the following four main aspects of the broad subject, "Implications of mass higher education."

    (*a*) **Structures of mass higher education.** To study whether the present structures can stand the strain or meet the tidal wave of the unprecedented expansion in numbers to which these were being subjected and to see whether new institutions, new programmes and new ways of thinking are needed. Purposes and structures of higher education in USA, UK, Western Europe, Eastern Europe, Canada and Japan were studied in detail.

(b) **Costs of higher education.** To study whether traditional methods of financing higher education are satisfactory for mass higher education, to study the cost-benefit analysis of higher education, to examine the relative costs and benefits of using various media (namely, normal lectures, correspondence courses, TV and radio, video-tapes, etc.), to examine the problems of economics of scale and to consider implications of considering education as an investment for the individual and the state.

(c) **Continuing education.** To study implications of the need of lifelong education, to study how to change the structures of universities to meet the needs of continuing education, to study the role of Open University and similar other organisations in continuing education and to study its relationship with adult education.

(d) **Students in mass higher education.** To study aims and objectives of the teaching staff, to have the students' views on curriculum development, to study teacher-student relationship, to consider present and future problems of graduate employment and to relate higher education to the needs of society.

4. Almost all the discussions were from the point of view of developed countries, but these are of still great interest to us in India for the following reasons :

(a) Higher education is rapidly becoming an international commodity. Problems of structures, costs, continuing education and student involvement are also of great interest to us.

(b) Comparative higher education is an academic discipline of great interest. Moreover, higher education everywhere is in such a dynamic state that one cannot get information on all aspects of its growth through books and journals and one has to get information at such international conferences to know the up-to-date position.

(c) With our limited resources, the problem of costs and benefits is of special interest to us and it is high time that our economists and educationists study this problem in all its implications in the context of economic, social, political and financial conditions in our country. We have certainly to optimise the use of our resources.

(d) The knowledge of most of the graduates trained 10-20 years ago has become out-of-date. In fact, in most cases it was out-of-date even when they took their degrees. With 70% of our people illiterate and with a large majority of our teachers, doctors, engineers, etc., not being on the frontiers of knowledge, the problem of continuing education is very important for us.

(e) We are likely to face educational problems which the developed countries are facing today, about 10-15 years later, and it will be good to learn from their mistakes as well as from their projections for the future.

(f) Even today India is, in some sense, in the stage of mass higher education. We had an elitistic system of higher education, but we are rapidly transforming it into an egalitarian system with our open admission policies in most universities and with reservation of seats for backward sections of the community in important institutions. In fact, in this respect, we are ahead of some of the developed countries.

(g) We have already over three million students in our universities and the growth rate is about 11-12% per year. The conventional system of higher education would be quite costly for the large increase in the number of students. We have to actively explore other methods of giving instruction right from now onwards.

(h) Sometimes asking the right questions is very important and the experience of the Western world may suggest the right questions to us.

2

STRUCTURES OF MASS HIGHER EDUCATION

1. Higher (or post-secondary) education is the system in which the inputs are secondary students and the outputs are the graduates and postgraduates who go into the labour market or even join the ranks of frustrated unemployed educated youngmen. The university structure is determined by the thinking, aims and ambitions of its faculty, by the goals of its patrons, namely, the society and the government, by the needs of its consumers, *viz.*, the students, by its own inertia or resistance to change and by the inner logic or need for consistency in its curricula and its programmes.

2. Universities are like green houses where various types of seeds grow into plants and are sent out into the world. Some green houses can be better than others. The green houses must be good and give healthy plants, otherwise the society may throw stones and destroy them. The universities must have the respect and love of society if they have to survive as useful instruments of change.

3. The university system must be acceptable to the society as such. In fact, it has to be satisfactory to the various elements of the society which very often pull in opposite directions. There are pressure-groups in society, both intellectual

and non-intellectual and both of these should have respect for the university system. In particular, the government and the members of the political decision-making bodies must have genuine respect for the universities and must support them in all possible ways. Higher education cannot grow satisfactorily in a society in which there is no deep feeling for the indispensiability of excellence in higher education for the progress of the society.

4. Higher education can be for the economic and industrial development of the country. Higher education can also be for enabling graduates to make better use of their leisure-time through intellectual pursuits. In Western societies, the problem of proper utilisation of leisure-time has become important with the prospect of a four-day working week. Higher education can also be meant to enable graduates to meet various challenges in a dynamic world and to produce in them strong adaptability to a changing society. Higher education can also be for civilising human beings, for producing a nobler race and for the proper evolution of mankind. Higher education can also aim at working for social justice and for producing an egalitarian society with complete equality of opportunity for every citizen.

5. One method of expansion of higher education is just changing of scale, *i.e.*, opening of more colleges and more universities of the present type with the same curriculum as at present. This is what expansion has implied in India. This leads to unemployment, because the labour market needs only a certain number of persons of a particular type. Our motto should be "More Means Different". We should have new courses, new curricula, new types of colleges, new types of universities and produce different types of graduates to meet the increasing needs of a diversified society. Unless we adopt this approach, certain needs of society will be over-fulfilled while others would be underfulfilled.

6. We should also ensure that "More Should Not Mean Worse". This actually happens when we increase the number of students, without increasing facilities or resources in the same ratio.

7. Higher education gives prestige to the graduates, but this prestige depends upon whether their education is vocational or non-vocational. This difference in prestige should go.

8. One important question to consider is whether we have terminal degrees in higher education after 2 years, 4 years, 6 years or 8 years, *e.g.*, whether we should have separate courses for those deciding to finish their education at BA/BSc level and altogether different courses for those intending to go for MA/MSc.

9. If a society can afford it, every one should be entitled to as much higher education as he needs or wants. Everyone is certainly entitled to facilities for continuing education at different periods in his life. In India we are at present committed to provide free and compulsory education till 14 years of age. Our ultimate goal should be to provide free, though not compulsory, education for all till the age of 22 years. Of course the goal is still far off.

10. There have been three great reports on educational system in the West, namely, the Robbin's report in U.K., report of the Wissencheftestrat in Germany and the colossal encyclopedia, already in 30 volumes, of the Carnegie Commission on higher education in U.S.A. All these reports have discussed in detail about increases in the size of higher education system, about problems of financing of the enlarged systems, about making an access to the system easier for all, about the cost-effectiveness of the system and about the relative efficiencies of the various alternatives. They have not discussed the necessary changes in the system, its functions in an evolving society and about the implications of "More Means Different".

11. Educational systems are strongly influenced by environment (E) and heredity effects (H), *i.e.*, by nurture and nature. There are three main environmental forces. One is customer demand (C), *i.e.*, the pressure of the students to get into the colleges and universities and the curricula which they want when they get in. A second force is manpower needs or the suction (S) of the labour market which influences the curricula.

Structures of Mass Higher Education

The third main force is the patron's influence (P), for ultimately the higher educational systems are influenced by the state which finances these systems.

12. There are two main heredity forces. One is inertia (I) or resistance of the system to change, and though annoying at times, it is useful, since the systems do need some stability and environmental forces are likely to change capriciously and arbitrarily. The second heredity force is inner logic (IL) of the system which is determined by the articles of faith of those who run it, by the needs of internal consistency, by the inevitability of certain subsequent decisions and by the need for identity for each system. These two heredity forces are more or less similar. If we do not like a force, we call it inertia and if we like it, we call it inner logic.

13. Our final model (due to Ashby) is the following :

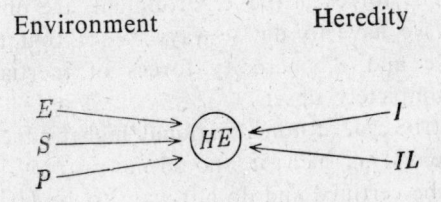

```
   Environment              Heredity

      E ─────⟶                ⟵───── I
      S ─────⟶    (HE)
      P ─────⟶                ⟵───── IL
```

The problem is how far higher education can reverse the arrows and influence the factors which are influencing it.

14. The balance between these forces differs in different countries. In the United States, the consumer demand has been a predominant influence and has been responsible for the large variety of courses and huge expansion in higher education. However, recently, the state has begun to influence higher education through federal grants or cuts in grants. In the USSR manpower needs and the state influence have played a predominant role, while inner logic has played only a secondary role. In Germany and UK, inner logic played very important role till recently, when students have begun to influence the system strongly.

15. In India, the labour market has determined student preferences. Legal, medical, agricultural, scientific, arts and commerce educations have been preferred at different times. The state has also done some manpower studies in technical and medical fields and has tried to influence educational trends in some areas. Inertia has been strong but the inner logic has been weak. There has been lack of balance with the labour market and this has led to frustration and unemployment. In arts courses, consumer influence has been strong, while the state has encouraged science courses. In technical and medical education, the state has had a controlling influence. The labour market has in recent years determined the shift of students' interest from engineering to medicine and from science to arts and commerce.

16. The traditional balance between the various forces has been upset in all countries and fascinating realignments are taking place, specially in view of the need for mass higher education. The forces of the environment are on the whole stronger and we have to devise ways to see that the balance between these and the heredity forces of inertia and inner logic is not completely upset.

17. The true aim of non-vocational higher education is to civilise people and as such it should not attract people who only want to be certified and do not want to be civilised. We may at most give certificates of having attended courses and of having done the assigned written work, otherwise we may be diverted from the true goal of civilization to the false goal of certification. For this purpose employers have to be reformed since they (including the governments) have done a great deal of harm to higher education by using degrees and diplomas as filters for their jobs while the degrees and diplomas are very often irrelevant to the jobs the students are going to fill.

18. One of the benefits of universal higher education may be that when every one has a certificate, the differentiating effect of certificates may disappear and the salary differentials between certified and un-certified persons may gradually diminish.

19. The object of higher education must be "to carry the student from the uncritical acceptance of orthodoxy to creative

dissent from values and standards of society" or "to impose a framework and at the same time encourage rebellion against it" or "to lift the student from the level of conventional moral reasoning to that of post-conventional level where he is deliberately challenged to re-examine assumptions, convictions and views which he previously took for granted" or "to keep our society pluralistic, humane and tolerant, open to alternative truths and able to distinguish prejudice from error". Seen in this light, we find that "the question is not whether we can afford universal higher education, but whether we can at all afford to be without it".

20. "The vocational purpose of higher education should be incidental and secondary. The principal reason for having universities and colleges should be concerned with expansion of civilisation, with the discovery of man's highest creative achievements, with the need in every generation to question and challenge what has been created and with the excitement of new discovery. The benefit is, or should be, the enlargement of culture and enlivening of minds. The reason for seeking mass higher education is the desire to extend to all who want it and can benefit by it an experience which has so far been confined to the few. The point in time at which a developed or developing country can afford mass higher education is simply that point at which this purpose has a sufficient political priority, *i.e.*, when people want it enough to sacrifice other things for obtaining it."

21. "We have damaged the cause of civilisation and culture by trying to convince people that they are 'good business' and that education has a yield as good as that of a jam factory, for the yield of studies (which while offering necessary training of the mind) have the direct vocational application might be expected to be greater than that of 'mere' cultural studies and it would follow therefore that merely cultural studies should be dropped from the curriculum. Why should any one except a school teacher or an actor study Shakespeare at an advanced level? Pop music is evidently more profitable than the classical music; the implications for music departments are thus clear. There is indeed no end to the nonsensical conclusions which can be reached by the assiduous servants of Mammon."

22. "Perhaps the greatest harm which has been done by the jam factory approach is to rob that part of education which is concerned with the summits of human achievements and with the boundaries which confront our vast ignorance and inadequacy with the awe and wonder which surround it. It is a pure silly thing, to attach to the discovery of the imperishable beauty of great works, to the profundity of philosophy, to the orderly subtlety of pure mathematics, money-value in increasing national production. The scholar in any society which claims greatness should be honoured for his own sake. If the civilisation in which we live does not give high enough importance to the things of the mind, we shall not make things better by pretending that scholarship is the servant of the affluent society."

23. Mass higher education, like mass production, is inconsistent with "hand-made" education. A great deal will have to be impersonal, using techniques such as programmed learning, video-tapes, TV, correspondence courses, computers, etc. However, education of the master craftsmen, the innovators in intellectual life and of pace-setters of cultural and moral standards must be personal and by masters whose own intellectual and cultural achievements are distinguished. This will imply elitistic education on a restricted scale, but no special institutions are necessary, for talent has to learn to work in a world of mediocrity.

24. Cost-benefit analysis should not be applied to higher education of the innovative mind, for such education may be even counter-productive, since such people may not go for high income careers and may even oppose increase of gross national product as a national goal. However, cost-benefit analysis has to be applied to the mass media education to ensure optimum efficiency.

25. A person can contribute to society through three skills, *i.e.*, skill in working with the ideas, skill in working with things, and skill in working with people. Our universities have so far tried to give first and second skills. Now our universities must give equal importance to the third skill of working with people.

26. The functions of a university are to bring about desirable modifications of intellectual, social and emotional be-

haviours of students, faculty members and citizens. These also include dissemination and modification of knowledge and of bringing about desirable social changes.

27. In principle, the desirable features of higher education are : open access, many open doors, open and not revolving doors, alternative paths within the system, mobility within the system, modules or course units, participation of students in decision-making, excellence of many different parts, place for research of genuine kind, research into higher education system itself, monitoring of statistics, internal self-government with representatives of students, professors and other faculty members and of the people in the world outside, cooperation with power centres of government authority, access to adequate resources and social justice for the less privileged.

28. The educational system can be called elitistic or minority when up to 20% students of the corresponding age group study in the system ; it becomes mass when 25-40% are in it and it becomes universal when more than 50% of the age group are there.

29. Higher education can be used in many different connotations, as for example, it can be used for any one of the following : post-secondary, advanced, excellent, further, continuing, etc.

30. The word 'structure' appears to give a static idea, whereas almost all educational structures are dynamic. Here we are concerned with teachers, students, teaching methods, internal government, external control and how each of these factors changes with time.

31. A horticultural model of higher education would be as follows :

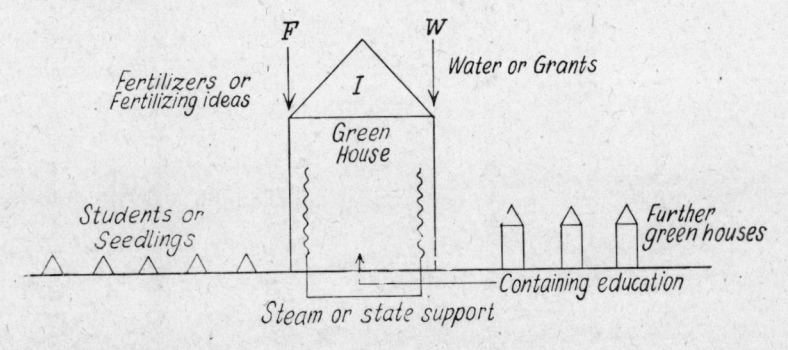

Heredity effects are there. We cannot convert lattuces into rubber plants. The system is a whole ecological system. Social justice cannot be done through higher education alone. It has to permeate the whole society. There can be many kinds of green houses and many kinds of inputs. For optimum use, costs and benefits are important. Every educationist has to be cencerned with economics of education. The educational system should sprinkle water and fertilizers not only on the seeds which are directly inside the system, but also on all those which are in the neighbourhood. Thus in the Open University, persons who are not registered as students can also listen to the educational programmes on the TV and benefit from them. We have to remember that every student is a living organism and has his own laws of growth.

32. In 1968-69, the percentage of the age group 18-22 enrolled in higher education in different countries were as follows :

U.S.A. (35%), Canada (28%), Sweden (16·9%), Japan (14·1%), France (13·9 %), Belgium (14·7 %), U.K. (13·5%), Germany (9%) and India (3%).

3

CONTINUING MASS HIGHER EDUCATION

1. One of the important facts to be taken into account by mass higher education is that of rapid obsolescence of knowledge. It is well-known that half the knowledge of some of the technologies becomes out-of-date within the life span of the working life of a technologist. In fact, half-life is in many cases of the order of 10 years, *i.e.*, half the knowledge acquired by a person becomes out-of-date in ten years' time.

2. Previously the half-life of knowledge was 100 or even thousands of years. The drugs prescribed 2,000 years ago continued to be valid till 100 years ago. Now the drugs taught to students may become out-of-date by the time they come out of the medical college.

3. Our doctors, engineers, teachers, etc. continue to pursue their vocations for about 40 years, though half of the knowledge they acquired in the educational system becomes obsolete in 10 years' time. They must go to colleges back again for extended periods of time to become students and get into rythm of learning if they have not to become harmful to society. This emphasises the need for continuing education.

4. One consequence of the obsolescence of knowledge is that the half-life of some institutions and even of some cultural

and moral values can also be measured in short periods of time.

5. "Therefore individuals have to reorient themselves during their life-time to new cultural and moral values as well as to new techniques." Also "if technology, concept of truth and concept of morality change within the individual's life-time, then adherence to one set of skills, one set of truths and one set of moral standards may leave the individual stranded, isolated and displaced before he reaches the middle age". Continuing education, both vocational and non-vocational, are therefore necessary for life.

6. The prejudice and built-in discrimination against adult student should go. Universities should cater to people of all ages. Higher education should not remain the monopoly of the youth. Education at all ages is required for realising the full potential of the individual.

7. Continuing education is necessary for better utilisation of the leisure which affluent societies are providing for their citizens and for the 'forced leisure' which developing societies still provide for their unemployed citizens. Boredom of increased leisure has to be avoided. Continuing education may point a way out of this boredom.

8. Employers demand updating knowledge on the part of the employees. Patrons want safeguards against obsolescence of knowledge of teachers, doctors, engineers, etc. Employees want to improve their earning prospects and the internal logic of the educational system itself demands continuing education.

9. One way of overcoming obsolescence is to pack more and more into initial education, increase the age of higher education to 23 or 25 years, so that the knowledge will last longer and longer. The other method is to shorten the initial period and give chances to the individual to return back to college at regular intervals. It is like the doctor giving a strong dose at once or giving one moderate dose in the beginning and the booster doses at regular intervals. However strong the initial dose, one dose will not do.

10. Let us assume that the time needed in a medical school is 5 years and the doctor returns for a 3-month course every

5 years in his working life of 40 years. The total time he will spend in the university would be 7 years and this will imply a 40% increase in resources. His working life will, however, decrease by 2 years and this will mean 5% reduction in his service to the society.

11. This example illustrates one reason why in spite of the felt need for further education, very little has been done. Further education is very expensive. In fact when teachers go to refresher courses in summer schools, their education is more expensive than that of regular students. Other reasons are inertia in every system and a pride in one's own knowledge which refuses to concede that one needs retreading, though one may concede that others need it.

12. It is obvious that if continuing education has to become a reality, conventional solutions will not do. We have to find cheaper means through correspondence courses and own-time study, etc. Correspondence courses in India and USSR and Open University in UK have demonstrated important ways for continuing education. These methods have two advantages, namely, these can be cheaper and at the same time do not withdraw persons from the productive work. Of course, these methods imply extra work both for teachers and students.

13. The Open University system also enables the good influence of one excellent teacher to spread. It also enables the teacher to concentrate and give one good performance instead of giving 100 indifferent ones. The difference is between a film performance and a theatre performance.

14. Successful continuing education will need large TV facilities. If we have a separate educational TV channel working for 18 hours a day, we can render 250 programmes of half-an-hour a week for 3 months in a year and thus in a year a total of 1,000 programmes can be shown on TV. Due to the large number of viewers, it may enable 5 million persons to benefit. At present in Britain, the Open University needs about 30 hours a week of TV time and the school broadcasts take about 20 hours a week. So about 40% of the channel time is already being utilised by the educational TV. Of course a new TV channel will mean a huge investment of 40 million pounds.

15. The conventional undergraduate course in UK costs £ 800 a year and with a separate channel, the cost may come to £ 20 a year which is quite reasonable. The gamble is a gigantic one, but national needs need national scale efforts.

16. Continuing education has to be on a massive scale. Small scale efforts may be self-defeating, as these will not be economical.

17. The major task consists in production of programmes. When other countries start open universities, some programmes in the same language can be exchanged and thus reduce costs.

18. Half the cost of Open University is on TV and radio broadcasting. Correspondence courses with study centres and books can be conducted at half the cost.

19. The age of continuing education is just beginning. The challenges and prospects are, however, both quite exciting.

20. Continuing education is a life-long education. It should reflect the values of society at a particular period of time. Each individual should get the chance for self-development and self-fulfilment and should be adequately compensated by being educated later in life if he missed educational opportunities in earlier life due to circumstances beyond his control.

21. We have to reconstruct higher education, taking into account continuing education. Universities have to have people of all ages. Old middle class dominating values have to give way. Education should be a uniting force. The universities should give continuing education a high priority. New university structures have to be devised for this purpose. Students have to be given two or three chances in life to make up for any deficiencies.

22. Continuing education need not be compulsory. The privileges of the few should become the rights of many, but these should not become the obligations of every one.

23. "As an enthusiast for continuing education once put it, there still are people who look upon education as they look upon an attack of measles. If you have had it once, you do not have to bother with it any more. Every one is concerned

about the drop-outs from schools and colleges. Not enough notice is being taken of the multitude that finish their formal education and then drop out altogether from learning".

24. "No one today disputes the need for keeping one's learning in continuous repair. In many areas, the content of knowledge becomes rapidly obsolete and even when it does not become obsolete, its relevance may have changed with the passage of time. There is no resting place for a man who would be educated. He has no choice but to opt for life-long education".

25. "The most important thing about education is appetite. Education does not begin with the university and it certainly ought not to end there."

26. "Since (due to student unrest) it seems to be impossible to educate the young, universities should develop the quality of fortitude and try to be of service to their unwilling clients after the period of formal instruction has ceased, and the young are no longer very young. Educationists have throughout the ages wanted to catch them young. They have now the obligation to catch them again when not so young".

27. Very often grown up persons are interested in programmes of learning outside the conventional ones, *e.g.*, programmes designed to improve one's own professional competence like programme of in-service training of teachers or programmes on computers or space technology or on ecology. Universities should begin by identifying the areas in which such courses are necessary so as to improve individual competence in the various professions.

28. The aims of continuing education can be :

  (*a*) improving the professional skills of the already educated ;

  (*b*) imparting productive skills to the uneducated ;

  (*c*) enabling already educated persons to develop new interests ;

  (*d*) the general stimulation of the intellectual and cultural life of the community ;

(e) enabling the student to learn on his own and thus dispensing with the necessity of his being taught subsequently.

29. Alternatively, the aims can be listed as follows :—

(a) promotion of the optimum functioning of individuals so that they realise their full potential and also contribute effectively to society ;

(b) inculcation of problem-oriented attitude and encouragement of the development of decision-making and leadership skills ;

(c) promotion of the optimum functioning of social, economic and political institutions so as to maximise their contribution to individuals and social development within the context of a democratic society ;

(d) helping the individual participate in a society characterised by complexity and rapid social changes.

30. In continuing education, a balance has to be struck between the provision of further opportunities to the already privileged class of educated citizens and the opening up of the avenues of human resources development on a mass scale by specific programmes designed for those outside the privileged groups.

31. The role of the university in continuing education arises from the following considerations :

(a) Continuing education activities would bring the university into closer contact with the outside world than its more formal undergraduate and post-graduate programmes can do.

(b) The possession of rich human resources in the form of its teachers and students and rich material resources in the form of library and laboratories, places on the university the responsibility of doing social good to the maximum extent possible.

(c) University can provide leadership to other organisations working for adult and continuing education.

(d) The university can encourage, within the community, habits of objective thought and investigation.

32. The universities can undertake programmes of the following types :
   (a) professional courses designed to update the knowledge of teachers, scientists, doctors, engineers, etc ;
   (b) courses in human relations, in leadership and executive skills and in decision-making processes ;
   (c) courses in humanities and liberal arts ;
   (d) courses of a remedial nature ;
   (e) action research and training on political and social problems ;
   (f) production of curricular materials for continuing education ;
   (g) training programmes for leaders in continuing education ;
   (h) education for political understanding ;
   (i) opportunities for cultural enrichment and creative use of leisure.

4

STUDENTS IN MASS HIGHER EDUCATION

1. Mass higher education will bring to universities those students who may not have earlier survived even the secondary school. These additional students will come from lower socio-economic strata of society with little family background of higher education. New strategies of teaching will have to be developed for the students.

2. These students will come to the university with great expectations unrelated to realities and the non-realisation of these expectations will cause anger, frustration and disillusionment. In fact it is almost axiomatic that mass higher education should mean frustration, some unemployment and anger.

3. We shall have to plan a diversity of courses for a diversity of students and introduce greater flexibility in our educational system.

4. Learning in mass higher education will have to have greater vocational significance, more personal significance and a realistic relevance to national and international issues.

5. The vocational courses in higher education will have to come within the degree structures of universities.

6. Students do not always want the super-market model of choices. They want to be advised and guided and at the same time to have their personal identity.

7. Students want interdisciplinary courses and opportunities of having contacts with students and staff of different departments.

8. Students feeling of belonging to an institution can come in an elitistic system, but it cannot come in mass education which will have to be for a major part impersonal.

9. Students' participation is necessary for overcoming alienation, but the participation in decision-making has to be more than token.

10. There will have to be more professional counselling in mass higher education and the counsellors will have to give necessary feed-back to the teachers. Senior students will have to be given responsibility of giving advice to juniors.

11. There will have to be employment advisory services on a larger scale. Advice will have to be given about post-graduate courses, about jobs being congenial to the students and about the time of entering jobs.

12. Multi-sandwich type of courses combining studies and work experience will have to be developed.

13. There will always be more politics in mass higher education than in the present minority higher education. This must be taken care of.

14. Students may have their separate conferences, but they will not be liberated unless they have joint conferences with faculty, government and others. They must take interest not only in student problems, but in all problems concerning higher education and the community. The feeling of student isolation must go. The students must also learn to agree among themselves. The vocal minority of students must not be able to dominate the silent majority.

15. Mass and continuing higher education may reduce the age-gap between the students and the teachers and may help in reducing present tensions.

16. All decision-making should be done jointly by students, academicians and university and government officials, otherwise confrontations are inevitable and decisions taken are unrealistic.

17. The real important problem today is that of student integration in the modern university. The student has to find personal happiness, personal fulfilment and commitment in a university environment and we have to find the conditions under which such an environment can be created. The aims of higher education and the aims of a congenial environment have to be reconciled. We need a great deal of experimentation and flexibility. Mild scepticism and cynicism have become the final attitudes in life of some student and teacher groups.

18. The students ought to have a new sense of values and they have to be given all the sympathetic understanding and love which they may have missed before coming to the university. The political rebellion of students requires a thorough discussion between students and teachers about the various ultimate purposes of education in society and this unfortunately is not possible in a mass education system.

19. Today students do not receive as much affection and attention from parents as the students of the earlier generation did. Very often they feel like orphans in their homes. When they come to universities, due to large number of students, they again feel individually neglected. The unrest appears very natural in this context.

20. Some of the students claim that the universities are being subjected to a number of hidden pressures reflected in the membership of the university bodies and in the orientation and the content of the curricula. They also contend that all research is related to industrial, military and political goals of the richer sections of the society. They contend that the ruling classes want to dominate the universities in order to achieve their own goals. The students even want to control the universities in order to remove the influence of these vested interests. The universities must assert their autonomy and freedom of thought to overcome this outside hidden control.

21. Universities have always fought for academic freedom and if efforts are made to remove one sort of influence, the effort should not result in installing other sets of political influences which may in fact further reduce the academic freedom of the university community.

22. In a Dutch student communication, it was written that each social activist should, in due time, steal, lie and use undemocratic means when he judges that he can help to stop dehumanisation of society. Students have to understand that means are as important as the ends.

23. The problem of the students in mass education is partly the question of how to recapture the finer qualities of university life which have been lost or are threatened in the larger university systems and how to restore the confidence of the younger generation in its teachers.

24. It is believed that student discontent and alienation can be removed by adopting better teaching methods, by organising better counselling and in general by resorting to all measures suitable to restoring a sense of belongingness in the university community and capable of bringing about an emotional and intellectual reconciliation between the student and his university.

25. Students often complain of the irrelevance of the curriculum. This criticism is very often hazy but there is no doubt that very often the curricula are framed in the interests of the teachers and not in the interests of the students. Teachers tend to include in the curriculum those topics in which they have specialised and these may very often be out-of-date and irrelevant to modern life.

26. The universities should allow free and frank discussion of all political, social and student problems, but the universities cannot allow direct action which may paralyse the life of the university itself and which may jeopardise the very values of intellectual freedom for which the university stands.

27. Sometimes there is no attempt to defend the present set of values of society which have evolved over centuries. These values are decried by some of the teachers and members of the society so much that students feel that there is a vacuum and

they want to move forward with revolutionary faith to fill in this vacuum. The new values for society have to emerge out of the old and not out of just empty air. This evolution will require hard work and cannot be done overnight. Students have to realise that even Lenin worked hard for thirty years to achieve success in the Russian Revolution.

28. Students have a right to make a contribution to the discussion on curricula. However this discussion will be meaningful only if they study hard all the issues involved. In fact such a study will itself be good motivated education. In the West, students in the age-group 22-25 form serious study groups to discuss these problems.

5

MASS HIGHER EDUCATION IN USA

1. The title of the book "Any Person, Any Study" by Ashby reflects the American attitude to universal higher education.

2. About 37% of 18—21 age-group go to universities and about 60% are enrolled for some form of post-secondary education. In California state, about 80% of this age-group go in for post-secondary education.

3. The idea is not to have universal attendance in higher education, but to have universal access to the system. This does not of course imply universal access to particular institutions.

4. In the seventies, 3 million more seats will have to be provided for additional students. These students will come from the lower-half of socio-economic strata of society and will also belong to the lower-half of scholastic ability. This will also imply increased representation of minorities and blacks in higher education.

5. The object is to provide universal higher education for two years beyond the school to every one and for this purpose 260 new two-year community colleges are going to be started. This will imply 14 years of free or subsidized education to every one in the USA.

6. Some other proposals of the Carnegie Commission on Higher Education are :—
   (a) Great increase in federal aid to higher education and in particular to medical or para-medical education.
   (b) Open access by 1980.
   (c) Greater employment opportunities to students.
   (d) Opportunities to re-enter college after some period of work-experience.
   (e) To save resources for higher education, one year should be cut from B.A., i.e., B.A. degree will be given 3 years after school.
   (f) An M. Phil. degree 2 years beyond B.A. should be provided.
   (g) In addition to Ph.D., there should be a Doctor of Arts degree directed to producing better teachers in universities.
   (h) 10 billion dollars should be saved by reducing a year in B.A. and 16 billion dollars extra should be provided by the federal government.

7. With increased federal support, the federal government wants to have more influence. This may lead to erosion of internal autonomy. The faculty unions have also started collective bargaining.

8. There is increased support from industry for higher education. Electronics industry in many places is situated around the universities. Thus the departments of electrical engineering at Stanford and Princeton have helped in the development of electronic industry around their campuses.

9. The universities are also accepting their responsibility for social reconstruction, as for example, for helping submerged groups to fight for their rights and by identifying themselves with the weaker sections of the Society. The universities have to be careful that they do not get politically-oriented in this process; that they guard their intellectual freedom and integrity and that they keep their vitality intact.

10. In California state every school graduate can join a two-year community college, everyone in the upper-third graduating class can join the state university and those in the top 12% are entitled to enter one of the nine campuses of

California University. This, however, has created 3 different classes of academic citizenship with consequent bitterness and frustration. The City University of New York tried a complete open admission policy in 1970 to enable blacks and Puerto Ricans to join. There were to be no failures in the first year. The attrition-rate was 35%, which was lower than the expected rate.

11. This new input of students below average ability has transformed the university. Academic credits are being granted for life or work experience, radically revised teaching-learning experiences are being explored, ethnic and women studies have been started. University can be for universal education but it has to change in the process of transition.

12. Universal higher education will mean higher budget, more government control, administration by trained management specialists and reduction in the influence of the faculty.

13. In 1970 in USA, about 64 million people were pursuing structured educational activities in the educational core (primary, secondary and post-secondary) whereas 60 million were in the 'educational periphery' which include (*a*) programmes sponsored by employers, business, government and industry; (*b*) proprietary schools, usually run for profit, including beauty schools, computer training, refrigeration schools, etc. ; (c) anti-poverty programmes such as Manpower Training and Development centres ; (*d*) correspondence courses ; (*e*) educational programmes for all ages—from Sesame Street to Sunrise Semester ; (*f*) adult education programmes in evenings. By 1977, it is expected that the number in the core would be 67 million as compared to 82 million in the rapidly growing periphery.

14. Twenty colleges in USA participate in a University Without Walls programme. There are no degree requirements, no prescribed time for getting a degree and unlimited opportunities, for learning outside the class-room and the campus. Each student designs his own individualised programme with guidance of a faculty adviser based on his own interests. The programme is based on two central principles : that relevant learning can take place in any location, in the class-room, on the job, in individual work projects and in

seminar discussions and that a variety of geographical locales can broaden a student's horizons and help him in gaining perspectives not possible within the confines of the classroom.

15. If enrolments go on increasing at the present rate, everyone of the age group 18-24 would be in higher education by the end of this century. This may not happen. However at least 70% of them are likely to be there. This means that about 16 million students may be in higher education in USA by the year 2000 A.D.

16. It is estimated that today one out of every six students in USA does not want to be a student. This means that about 1 million unwilling students are there. By 2000 A.D. this number may become two-and-a half million and such a large number of unwilling students may damage the system. This is what is already happening in India.

17. Today about 2 million students fail to complete the degrees for which they enrol. In 2000 A.D., this number may rise to $6\text{-}7_m$ million and this will be such a tremendous wastage for which the taxpayer may not be willing to pay.

18. The cost per student is going up and the goals of higher education for everyone are not always clear. This decreased productivity may cause problems.

19. There are 2 million students in two-year community colleges, 2½ million in the 1,500 four-year colleges and 2½ million in 160 universities. They had different purposes, but gradually 2-year colleges are becomings institutions preparing for 4-year colleges and 4-year colleges are becoming institutions preparing for graduate schools. The primary purposes of 2 and 4 years college therefore remain unfulfilled.

20. American higher education system is characterised by VARIETY, DIVERSITY, FLEXIBILITY and TRANSFER.

6

MASS HIGHER EDUCATION IN UK

1. Britain is still far away from mass higher education. USA has emerged from mass higher education and is going in for universal higher education. The proportion of age-group 18-21 in British post-secondary institutions (universities, polytechnics and colleges of education) is 13.5% while in USA it is 37%. The UK may have 8,35,000 students in 1981 but still she will be far away from the position of USA in 1971. It would require about 1½ million students in 1981 to reach the present US percentage and this is a long way from the present figure of about 400,000.

2. Working class children, women and racial minorities are under-represented in UK higher education. Working class children may even become rejects of mass higher education. Even polytechnics are becoming middle class institutions.

3. Counselling can help only to a limited extent. More flexibility is needed in changing of courses and changing of institutions. Community colleges within commuting distances of working class population centres are needed to encourage them to go to higher education. Even in Berkeley, there are community colleges, state university and California University and a large number of students can make transfers between

these three organisations. In UK also differentiated structures are necessary.

4. No country, not even USA, can afford to train 30% of its population in age-group 18-22 according to standards of Harvard or Princeton. In Britain, all 45 universities and 30 polytechnics cannot become distinguished first-rate comprehensive universities. Of course any differentiation may invite opposition, but for mass education, this differentiation has to come one day.

5. Mass higher education may result in graduate unemployment or underemployment. Ultimately, the result will be that all school teachers will have to be graduates; nursing would become a university subject and similarly, in other vocations, higher academic qualifications may be required than at present.

6. Half the grants in UK are given to those who can support themselves. These are given through local authorities. The Vice-Chancellors wanted the government to increase the fees of all students, but this would have meant the government giving money to the local authorities to be given to the students to be passed on to the universities. The government was more willing to give direct grants, so that it could have more control on the universities. The fees for overseas students were, however, increased against the wishes of the academicians and without consulting the UGC or the universities.

7. Mass higher education should not be a middle-class privilege. Every person should have a basic entitlement to free higher education and beyond that he should meet his expenses through loans or from his own pocket.

8. In UK there is really no long-term planning for development. Polytechnics are proceeding towards university models and are not realising the objectives of serving the community around them.

9. UGC in Britain was started in 1919 to advise government about giving grants to the universities. It was under Treasury and not the Ministry of Education. It acted as a buffer between the government on the one side and the autonomous universities on the other. In 1946 it was asked to

play a more positive and clearer role in higher education. However, there were tremendous increases in grants and the Public Accounts Committee wanted accountability. The Treasury resisted these demands, but the strains began to appear in early sixties. In 1962, the grants were reduced and the UGC recommendations were not accepted. The UGC members threatened to resign, but were persuaded to stay on. In 1963, the UGC was placed under the Ministry of Education. PAC and Controller General of Accounts wanted access to UGC records. This was accepted. The Controller General agreed not to interfere in academic matters, but the academic and financial matters are closely interlinked.

10. The UGC in UK has carried out studies on cost-effectiveness, space-utilisation, faculty-time use, expenditure on teaching and research and other important problems of higher education.

11. There is a demand that all UGC meetings should be open and basis of its discussions must be known. The danger of government control must be resisted. The UGC must do long-term planning, develop management systems and may do even the dirty work of budget control.

12. The membership of the Board and UGC should go beyond all professors (who are always in favour of the establishment) and high business people (some of whom should be replaced by labour representatives) and should include some parliamentary representatives.

13. The fees in UK are of the order of £ 100 per year, while the expenditure per head is £ 600-700 per year. There is little guidance and students have an instinct of what they want. This is illustrated by the students voluntarily shifting from science to arts and social sciences in recent years.

14. The government has decided to give more development funds to the polytechnics for development, partly because the universities are not as amenable to the government's advice as the government would like them to be. There are also strong demands for comprehensive universities, including present universities, polytechnics and colleges of education under their umbrellas.

15. In UK the birth rate was maximum in 1947. It fell down to a minimum in 1955 and again rose to the maximum in 1964. At this point they are recruiting students from 1955 birth year and as such the demands on higher education are likely to go up significantly in the near future.

16. Now everybody wants to go in for higher education. It requires strength of character for some one to say : "No, I would not go in for higher education".

17. The number of students in higher education doubled in sixties and is again going to double in the seventies. About a dozen new universities have been started since 1960. The Open University was started in 1969 and may do for the British higher education what the Land Grants Colleges did for the American higher education.

18. Universities in UK have responded to the challenges of the time and it is not true to say that they have not been sensitive to demands on them, in spite of the fact that the universities are still regarded as communities of scholars.

19. The overall staff student/ratio is 1 : 8 ; about 25% students go in for science, 20% for arts, 20% for social sciences and the rest go in for other studies.

20. The earliest, *i.e.*, Oxford University was founded in 1167 and the Open University was started in 1969. UK has now 45 universities, 30 polytechnics and 140 colleges of education. Fees are low and 80% students are state-supported. Others can also earn enough to maintain themselves.

21. Entry to universities is very narrow. The system is elitistic and for an egalitarian system, tremendous expansions in enrolment are necessary.

22. There is the three-tier system of higher education with universities, polytechnics and colleges of education. The universities are expensive to the government because of heavy research commitments. Polytechnics cost less and the Open University is the cheapest, because so far there are no build-

ings or research commitments. The universities are prestigious; polytechnics are businesslike and colleges of education are professionals. There are in addition a large number of post-experience colleges for continuing education.

23. The 45 universities are not equal. Each has some famous departments and some universities have more famous departments than others.

7

MASS HIGHER EDUCATION IN FRANCE AND OTHER WEST EUROPEAN COUNTRIES

1. To understand the position in France, we consider it in relation to three basic concepts, namely, those of structures, values and tactics. The structure refers to relationships between parts of a system. The relationships are not immutable, nor they are necessarily permanent. We are interested in "who tries to change the relationship between parts", "who can change" and "how he can change this relationship". As for values, a system does not possess values. It is the people who cherish values. Every system can be geared to work for those values which people want. As for tactics, we have to know what limitations existing structures put on a system, what parts can be most easily changed, what relationships are easiest to modify and which modifications will produce maximum desirable results.

2. The French higher education is highly centralised. The Centre influences most and is influenced least by its parts. This fact has had most profound effects on changes in the system.

3. In France, mass higher education has gone far without any body trying consciously for it. This is due to structural

relationship between secondary school system and university system whereby every student who completes the secondary school is automatically entitled to enter the university. The consequence has been that students have flooded the universities. During the last 15 years the number of students trebled. The number of university students in 1967 was equal to the number of secondary students in 1956. New universities have been started, but there is overcrowding in all the universities.

4. We state three propositions and then examine them :

    (*a*) Mass student intake implies differentiation.

    (*b*) The present French system is opposed to differentiation and specialisation.

    (*c*) This contradiction leads to difficulties and strains in the system.

5. Mass intake implies differentiation in the population of the students which enter the university. The cultural homogeneity which used to be there in the past has been lost. On the other hand, massifying higher education means withdrawal of a section of the population of the age group 18-22 from the labour market and from training in skills and apprenticeships which this population would have otherwise received. As such, the university also gets demands on it for this type of training within the university system. The universities will have to be therefore specialised within higher education.

6. There are strong vested interests in a centralised system and they are opposed to specialisation which implies local autonomy. A centralised system means national uniformity in curricula and so local initiative cannot play an important role.

7. The system is constantly under strain. The V.C. is, in a sense, a government representative and has no financial control which is exercised by the ministry and its officials. Curricula are centrally-controlled and there is no selection of students. There is no internal flexibility and there is no adaptation to local needs. Discontented elements cannot go to any other systems. Even in schools, Catholic schools have to follow the same curricula. Innovation and initiative are strictly inhibited under these conditions.

8. Under these conditions, the students and the faculty cannot influence the system from within. The only way is to get control of the political machinery and then change the system from without. The faculty and the students tried to do this in France in 1968. There had to be a head-on political attack, since in France education is a political process.

9. The leftist parties in France have been in political disarray. The parliamentary system has not worked very well. The ministry of education has thus escaped the indirect influence of public opinion. The ministry of education is the biggest employer in the world, second only to the Red Army. In Italy, there is a similar problem but political parties are against differentiation. The argument is that there should be no second class institutions, for this may mean second class citizens and so uniformity must prevail.

10. The French system has shown enormous capacity to resist changes in spite of increase of numbers.

11. Just as in France, enrolments in higher education in all other countries of Western Europe have more than doubled in 10 years.

12. The increase in resources for higher education has been significant ; in fact many times more rapid than the increases in enrolments. So in these countries, more has not meant worse.

13. In most countries the system is elitistic, though conscious and deliberate steps towards egalitarian systems are being taken.

14. The major influence in recent years has been that of the consumers, namely, the students. They have secured 20-33% share in decision-making bodies.

15. Standards have been a casualty in some places, but very often it is the vested interests who have shouted most about maintenance of standards with the real purpose of maintaining status quo.

16. In one country, a university was started with all possible innovations, but it turned out to be a failure.

17. In Spain, there was a brief peirod in which the government fell in line with educational growth when Parliament endorsed a comprehensive new Education Act in June 1970. However, soon after this the government failed to provide the money needed for the reforms and forgot the universal truth that the more you educate people, the more freedom of expression is expected by them. In 1971, the government decided to go back on its plans, dismissed 200 non-conformist teachers, set up juries to punish sins against national loyalty and gave teachers a clear mandate. "Be scholarly, be studious, but beware of your political behaviour".

18. In Sweden there have been many innovations. One of these is the state-financed 'school for life', which students may enter and leave on a continuing basis throughout their lifetime.

19. Some important studies in higher education have been carried out in Belgium. The number of students increased from 58,000 in 1960 to 133,000 in 1970 and will probably be about 210,000 in 1985. It is expected that the number of women students will increase much more rapidly in future under the influence of the growing importance of para-medical and higher educational studies for them.

20. It is expected that the percentage of the age-group 18-21 in higher education will increase from 16% in 1970 to 25% in 1985 for male students and from 8·5% to about 15·4% for female students.

21. In 1962-66, about 30-40% of the students belonged to the highest socio-professional groups and about 50% were of middle class origin. Only 10-20% belonged to lower socio-economic classes.

22. The ideal proportion will be when each socio-economic group is represented in higher education in the same proportion in which it is represented in the population as a whole. If the index of perfect proportional representation is taken to be 100, then index of the highest professional classes was 1825 in 1934 and 1,263 in 1966. For the higher management group it was 860 and 560 respectively and for commerce and business it was 409 and 215 respectively. Manual workers

index rose from 100 to 209, of employees in general from 23 to 24. These figures show that while the share of the upper groups is decreasing and that of the lower groups is increasing, the discrepancies are still large.

23. Though the middle-class students also join some of the professional and managerial courses, the overwhelming majority of those who actually enter these professions belongs to the families which had already been working in these areas.

24. It has been concluded that in a working class environment, some form of knowledge of the academic sphere has to exist in order to stimulate the desire for further education.

25. It has been proposed that a student wanting to register at a comprehensive university should be asked to present and defend his application in an interview with the Board of Admission on the basis of his secondary school record. He should also be able to discuss critically the results of the aptitude test to which he would have been subjected and he would have to procure evidence that he knew about the career possibilities offered to graduates in his chosen field of study. The Admission Board would advise the student, but the final decision will be that of the student.

26. Opinion polls have shown that students of lower socio-economic groups and students of humanities favour open access to higher education, while others prefer selective admissions.

27. The recent educational developments in Western Germany, with special reference to student's participation are discussed in detail in the essay on 'Higher Education, and Research in West Geamany' included in this book.

8

MASS HIGHER EDUCATION IN EASTERN EUROPE

1. Higher education in most of the countries of Eastern Europe is on the Soviet pattern. About 2—7% of their populations are in higher education, with Soviet Union leading with 7%.

2. In the Soviet Union, there are 46 million secondary students, 5 million vocational secondary students and only 3·6 million students in universities. This represents the degree of selection at the end of the school.

3. The Soviet higher education system has a dilemma to face. The government wants an egalitarian system while man-power planning and needs of production force it to choose. Thus in Soviet schools, children must learn different languages according to the choice of the government and not according to their choice. This conflict between needs of an egalitarian system and the production ideals of socialism cannot but produce unavoidable tensions in the system.

4. During 1951-70, the secondary enrolments increased by seven times, while college enrolments only became double.

5. The motto of the Soviet system is to produce better men for a better communist society.

6. The dream of every student in Soviet Union is to become a doctor or an engineer or a designer as everywhere else in the world, but then who will build houses ? So every one cannot go in for higher education.

7. In spite of all efforts, 60% of students in higher education come from 10% of the population, since even here the system can be made to work for you, if you know how to work it properly.

8. A Polish education text recently stated the objectives of higher education to be as follows :—
   (a) to prepare students for participation in building up a society ;
   (b) to train specialists for production ;
   (c) to develop national cultural programmes.

9. Between 1945-58, in Poland there were 211 government edicts and 1,350 piecemeal reforms in education system. This shows the evolution of the educational system.

10. In Eastern Europe, the inner logic of the university has to be reconciled to the inner logic of the political regime.

11. There is a deliberate effort to see that higher education does not result in creation of new classes of intelligentsia. Thus admissions cannot be made on merit alone. Family background has to be an important consideration.

12. Children of teachers should get admissions on merit, but they get only a limited quota of seats. Teachers cannot be very happy in such a system.

13. There is a system of bonus marks for manual workers in Poland and Czechoslovakia, so that their children get preference in educational system. Still no child turns up for certain courses like music.

14. The structure of applications for various courses is revealing. The effort to change human nature in less than one generation is proving self-defeating.

15. It has been shown here that planning does not necessarily solve problems of unemployment. Still highly qualified people go in for jobs requiring low qualifications.

16. It has been shown that big transformations in attitude may take more than one generation to be achieved.

9

MASS HIGHER EDUCATION IN CANADA

1. The most important development in recent times in Canada has been the report of the Wright Commission on post-secondary education for the Ontario province of Canada. Its draft report was published in 1972 for inviting public comments.

2. The Commission had two major concerns, viz., to control costs and to complete the transition from the elitistic system to mass post-secondary education and in this process to wipe out discrimination.

3. The Commission formulated the following principles :

(*a*) There should be *universal accessibility* to post-secondary education *at all ages*. Life-long education and part-time attendance must be encouraged and new ways of delivering educational services must be found.

(*b*) All educational services must be *open* to the public and indeed integrated with the general cultural activities of the community. Public libraries, museums, art galleries and science centres should be treated as part of the community's educational services.

(c) There should be great *diversity* of admission standards, lengths of programmes, bridging-over courses and flexibility in course structures.

(d) Post-secondary education should be sufficiently *responsive* to new social demands and also be prepared to abandon those that are no longer necessary. All innovations must be encouraged.

(e) There should be easy *transferability* from institution to institution, from one programme to another and from one profession to another.

4. The recommendations of the Commission included the following:

(a) Leave facilities for all employees wishing to pursue post-secondary education.

(b) Substitution of practical experience gained in factories for formal practical experience in laboratories.

(c) Credits for courses in industry and government.

(d) Eligibility of part-time students for financial assistance.

(e) Legislation to allow an employee to forgo a certain percentage of his salary every month in lieu of guaranteed study-leave at regular intervals.

(f) Permission to labour unions to bargain for study benefits instead of salary increases.

(g) Special grants to be given to libraries in communities beyond commuting range of post-secondary educational institution for the benefit of correspondence course and open university students.

(h) Access to all citizens to libraries of colleges and universities.

(i) Creation of a 'University of Ontario' to provide educational services via television, radio and correspondence; to provide a testing and evaluation service on demand and to award degrees on the basis of this testing, without requiring formal course work.

(j) Provision of evening courses for part-time students.

(k) Development of refresher courses at all levels to enable persons at 'lower' levels to acquire competence to go to 'higher' levels.

(l) No bar on account of sex or age to any student for admission to any course of studies or for eligibility for financial aid or for rights of access to student-centres, etc.

(m) Grant to a person who does not opt for post-secondary education, equivalent to the subsidy by the government, to enable him to purchase any cultural or educational services he wants.

5. The recommendations involve the creation of three sectors of post-secondary education, viz., universities, colleges and 'open-sector'. The open sector is to encompass all those institutions that now provide informal education such as libraries, theatres, art museums and art galleries. According to the Commission : "If education, or learning is viewed as an individual activity, there cannot be any doubt about their educational contribution. The fact that such an activity is often undertaken without any of the usual rewards associated with general education is perhaps even greater reason to include it under an educational umbrella. Further we see these institutions and the services they now provide, as major avenues through which citizens of all ages can gain access to highly flexible and varied set of eductional experiences. To emphasise these two aspects of these services, we have called this sector of post-secondary education, as the open sector."

6. In its recommendations, the Commission wanted to be fair to :

(a) **the society** by making individual beneficiaries of education to pay half the cost ;

(b) **the student** by separating research and teaching cost, so that the student will pay half of the teaching cost only;

(c) **the students** and parents by providing grants or loans to poor students;

(*d*) **the person with no formal qualifications** by easy entry requirements;

(*e*) **the person who cannot leave his job** by providing the open university;

(*f*) **the person who wants education of a non-institutional kind** by creating an 'open sector' which would include the open university, libraries, museums, galleries and other cultural elements and by providing grants to persons pursuing their education by such manner;

(*g*) **the person who has no secondary degree or diploma** by granting degress or diplomas in recognition of experience and self-education and to make laws against discrimination of such degrees;

(*h*) **Society** by weakening the closed shop of the professors and by insisting on periodic re-certification.

7. The *criticisms* of the report are as follows :

(*a*) Commission is trying to do too many things in one package deal.

(*b*) Standards of education are likely to fall.

(*c*) It is not clear what the total cost of the system would be to the State.

(*d*) The report is anti-university, and anti-degree.

(*e*) Separation of research from teaching shows a lack of understanding of both.

(*f*) The implementation will require more bureaucratic control and result in less university autonomy.

(*g*) The universities will lose the four freedoms they have enjoyed so far, namely, the freedom to determine what should be taught, the freedom to determine who shall be taught, the freedom to determine who would teach and the freedom to distribute resources as it thinks fit.

(*h*) Though the universities have to spend a great deal of time in self-government, the universities will not be able to pursue excellence in an environment of restrictions.

8. One of the above proposals resembles the proposal recently made by Mr. Naik for India. The student should pay for the cost of his education and only poor students should be supported by the government. The first argument, of course, holds for the minority education where only certain classes are getting the benefits of higher education and all tax-payers are paying for it.

10

MASS HIGHER EDUCATION IN JAPAN

1. Japan has a 6-3-3-4 'single-track' system of education. The higher education institutions in Japan are the following :
    (*a*) Universities.
    (*b*) Junior colleges.
    (*c*) Technical colleges.
    (*d*) Miscellaneous colleges.

The enrolments of the corresponding age-groups are 99% in elementary and lower secondary classes, 85% in upper secondary classes and 26·8% in universities and junior colleges. There are 14 lakh students in universities and 13 lakhs in miscellaneous schools as against the figure of 30 lakhs in India.

2. There are 389 universities in Japan, of which 75 are national, 33 municipal and 281 are private. Some universities have less than 20 teachers and some have more than 1,500. The total enrolment has increased by more than 200% in the last 10 years.

3. There are 486 junior colleges of which 22 are national, 32 municipal and 432 are private. In the last 10 years, 196 new colleges have been established and the enrolment has increased by 300%. Out of 275,000 students in all the junior colleges, 83·1% are women as compared with 18·3% female

students in the universities. In junior colleges, women students study home economics, teacher training and literature. Very few women students go in for science, agriculture, law and economics.

4. More than 80% of 63 technical colleges are national. The total enrolment is 46,000. The technical colleges are 5-year institutions and provide technical education to lower secondary graduates. Industrial colleges train technicians and mercantile training colleges train students for transportation and business.

5. Miscellaneous schools provide for up-to-date and indispensable techniques for specialised professions, home-making and general living. The enrolment is 13 lakhs, out of which about 10 lakhs are women.

6. Students' demands in Japan are mostly concerned with curriculum improvement, withdrawal of raises in tuition fees, self-management of student halls and dormitories, students' participation in university administration, withdrawal of student punishment, government financial support for private universities, reform of university entrance examination system, etc. In practice, these demands have led to informal confinement and impeachment of teachers and to political demonstrations.

7. The percentage of distribution of faculty position is as follows : Professors 31%, Asstt. professors and lecturers 37% and assistants 32%. This forms a 'chimney' style as contrasted with pyramidal structure in India where the percentage may be 4, 16 and 80 respectively. In the Japanese system, the chances of promotion are high and the psychological stability is good. A survey undertaken by the Japanese National Institute for educational research during the period of student unrest showed that 70% of the university teachers desire to become university teachers again, if they were reborn. The chimney type of academic hierarchy has also the merit that the teachers are able to settle down to do research for long periods of time.

8. The demerits of the chimney type of academic hierarchy are the following :

    (*a*) appointment of a university teacher on the life tenure system at an early age can lead to mis-evaluation of his academic ability,

    (*b*) the seniority principle works in practice,

    (*c*) interchange of teachers between different universities does not take place,

    (*d*) the age distribution can be uniform.

9. In India, we have a pyramidal structure, recruitment to permanent service at an early age, principle of seniority in promotions and tenure system from the beginning. This has the disadvantages of no incentives for work and frustration on account of non-promotion.

10. In Japan about 65% of university teachers have their primary interest in research, about 27% have their primary interest in teaching and other 8% are interested partly in both. Some teachers want to do research in pedagogy and innovations and are unwilling to do research for the sake of research only.

11. The grading system in Japan is not working satisfactorily for the following reasons :

    (*a*) Teachers have to grade a large number of students without additional payment,

    (*b*) strictness in evaluation will imply that the teachers will have to teach the same students again and this would imply evaluation of larger number of answer books,

    (*c*) teachers prefer to evaluate on the basis of attendance as they have a suspicion that routine examinations measure only the quantity of knowledge.

    (*d*) the legal provision of preparatory learning for 2 hours outside class per lecture is neither observed nor insisted upon,

    (*e*) a student has to obtain minimum grades in every subject and no averaging is done.

12. The employers do not give much importance to the university education as it has almost become universal. Sometimes they recruit undergraduates and give them some initial training under their firms while they are still students. The performance of the students is more or less same as at the entrance examination and it is thus believed that in Japan students face difficulty only in getting admission to a university and not afterwards.

13. Young people have a sense of deep void in their hearts. They have a feeling of meaninglessness and loss of will and powerlessness. In fact, political movements of radical students may be interpreted as symptoms of the students trying to get out of such a state of mind. Teachers are interested in research and not in students and as such under the present circumstances, the chances of improvement in teacher-student relationships are not high.

14. The Central Council for Education in Japan has submitted a five-point proposal for education reforms. The points concern popularisation of higher education, specialisation and integration of curricula, emphasis on both teaching and research, administrative autonomy for each higher educational institution and nation-wide planning.

15. The Central Council has proposed diversification of higher education, improvement of curricula, improvement of teaching methods, open university system, functional separation between teaching and research, reformation of graduate schools, rationalisation of administrative organisations, improvement of the quality of the teaching staff, additional financial support, national planning of higher education, improvement of life-environment of students and improvement of the examination system for university entrance.

16. There are three types of curricula in the university: type A which provides for those coming into wide range of occupations, a general and broadbase of knowledge, type B provides for a systematic academic training for those who intend to go into specific professions in which academic skills are needed while type C trains specialised personnel like teachers, artists and athletes.

17. Junior colleges have a two-year programme, mostly for women.

18. It is proposed that graduate schools should be separated from undergraduate departments, but should be within institutions which are adequately equipped for research, because graduate schools compete with the undergraduates in

facilities and staff and give more attention to the graduate programmes.

19. The research centres would train academic research workers and award doctorate degrees. There will be an interchange of students between the graduate schools and the research centres.

20. It is expected that by 1980, 90% of the students of the age-group will be in upper secondary education and the enrolment in higher education will reach 50% before it reaches 100% in the upper secondary schools.

21. Employers have been demanding that there should be some sort of grading among institutions of higher learning to facilitate recruitment by them of graduates.

22. In one university, no graduation certificate is given. The student has to continuously evaluate himself and leave the university whenever he likes.

23. The present educational system and the proposed system are shown in the following figures.

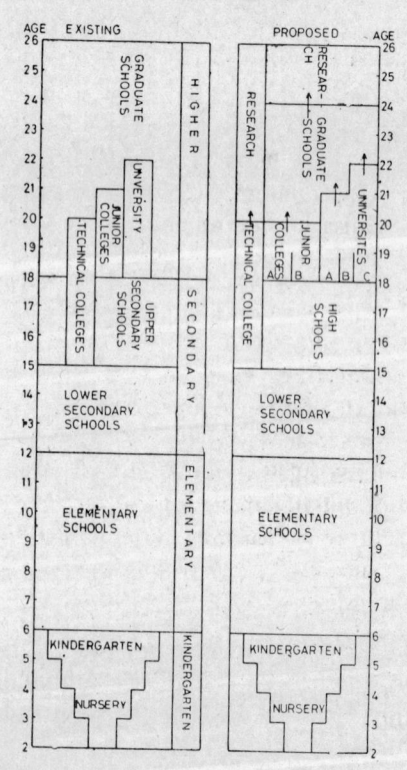

11

MASS HIGHER EDUCATION IN CHINA

1. Though there is universal informal education in China in the sense that everyone is involved in some form of education or re-education through Mao's thought-study groups, literacy classes, part-time study programmes, correspondence education, etc., there is no mass higher education as the number of students in universities is extremely limited and the Chinese do not want to develop an over-educated elite class.

2. Chinese education has the following characteristics: (*a*) inculcating a spirit of serving the people and serving others before self, (*b*) application of knowledge gained to the farms and factories, (*c*) teaching by experienced farmers and workers, (*d*) deep involvement of the community in the educational process, (*e*) education to serve the political goals of the party, (*f*) emotional training against all forms of exploitation, (*g*) collective instead of individualistic education (*h*) cooperation rather than competition in learning, (*i*) inculcating a sense of dignity of labour among the teachers and (*j*) equal opportunities for all and faith in group wisdom.

3. After secondary school, every one has to spend at least two years (normally 3—5 years) in manual labour on the farm, factory or the army. Most remain workers for their lives; only

a few estimated at 100,000 compared with 900,000 before the Cultural Revolution (1966-1969) are selected by the working units for higher education. There is no open-door admission to higher education, as demanded by our students. Higher education is not a right, but is a privilege to be earned by hard work.

4. The Chinese do not want three-door bureaucrats who pass from the door of the home to that of the school and college to the door of the office without any contact with life. Their system of education ensures this.

5. The universities are run by elected revolutionary committees. At Peking University 39 members of this committee in 1971 included 7 members of the people's Liberation Army, six workers, six members of political cadre, nine teachers, seven students, 3 workers from university-run factory and one representative of faculty and staff families. The chairman is a political cadre and the vice-chairman is an academician who looks after day-to-day work of the university.

6. To be admitted, a student must be at least 20 years old and qualified in political ideology as shown by "mastery of Mao's thoughts to forge close links with the masses and by his willingness to serve the people." He must have been an outstanding production worker in the production unit in which he may have been working after secondary school and must have been nominated and at least recommended by it.

7. At a university, the students' schedule of work is as tightly controlled as in public schools in India. Examinations are just meant to find what remedial action is to be taken but no grades are recorded. No student ever fails ; all cooperate to make sure that not a single class-mate is left behind. After education, the student must return to the production process from which he came.

8. The aim of the new educational policy is to gradually eliminate the "culturally isolated intellectual and expert classes" from society so that the masses and workers will themselves be in contact with the knowledge and skills earlier only available to these elite experts.

9. University curricula are being "integrated with production" to reflect Mao's doctrine that universities should combine "education, production and research". Thus Futan University has completely dropped the traditional curriculum in literature and science and replaced it with such subjects as electronics and optics. The university factories built by the staff, students and outside experts and workers produce equipment from quartz-tungsten lamps to logic circuits for third-generation computers.

10. University faculty members have been asked to change their attitudes and have been "re-educated" (politically) in special schools. Specialist doctors and engineers working for classes have been obliged to work for the masses.

11. Science is regarded as a collective group activity in which theory and practice must always be united to serve production.

12. The formal educational process has been shortened from 6 years to 4 years in secondary schools, from 5 years to 3 years at the university and from 6 years to 3 years in medical colleges.

13. Students and teachers spend 1 to 2 months every year studying production processes in farm and factories.

14. There are about 100 million children in the primary schools, about 10 million in secondary schools and only 1 million in the universities. This compares with 60 million in primary schools and 3·5 million in universities in India.

15. The violent opposition to the examination system in China is indicated by the following statement : "The old examination system is most dangerous and harmful to our socialistic causes. It places not proletarian but bourgeois politics in command. The system shuts out many outstanding children of workers, poor and middle class peasants and opens the gate wide to the bourgeois to cultivate its own sucessors. The system encourages acquisition of individual fame, wealth and position."

16. The part-work part-study educational institutions are popular in China and have helped in diminishing the differen-

ces between mental and physcial labour and have helped the students to learn from both types of teachers, viz., the classroom teachers and the worker-tutors, thus facilitating the all-round moral, intellectual and physcial development of the students.

17. A characteristic Mao statement often quoted during the cultural revolution was : "I shall always believe that the majority of intellectuals, both within and outside the party, are basically bourgeois." Mao first tried to persuade intellectuals to take interest in manual work and he failed ; then he tried to graft a worker's personality over the intellectual personality and he failed ; he sent workers to universities without changing the intellectuals as teachers and he again failed and finally he sent workers and also sufficiently re-educated teachers to change this attitude in the universities and he has apparently succeeded. This has obvious lessons for India.

12

THE OPEN UNIVERSITY

1. Motivated by the desire to provide higher education to those who cannot afford to leave their jobs, this university was established on 30-5-69 as an independent autonomous body to provide education of university and professional standards for students and to provide for the educational well-being of the community generally.

2. The idea of a "University of the Air" was first publicly discussed by Mr. Harold Wilson in 1963 ; a British Government White Paper was published in 1966 ; a planning committee was appointed in 1967 and its report was submitted and accepted by the government in early 1969. In January 1971, 24,000 students began to study the foundation (first level) courses in arts, science, mathematics and social sciences for B.A. degree. In 1972, another foundation course in technology, together with some 20 second-level courses were introduced. In 1973, third level courses, post-experience courses and post-graduate programmes are going to be introduced. There will be no foundation course in the faculty of education.

3. For B.A. degree, six credits and for B.A. (Hons.) degree 8 credits are required. For each of the degrees, two of the credits obtained must be at the foundation level. The two extra credits for honours degree must be at the third level.

Students with certain qualifications obtained at other universities (called conventional universities) may be awarded up to three credit exemptions.

4. The system has a great deal of flexibility. A student may choose courses from one faculty only or from many faculties. Each course which is produced by a combined team of academic staff, BBC staff and educational technologists is self-contained and leads to award of a full or half (in exceptional cases to 1/3rd and 1/6th) credits. Students can take up to two full credit courses in a year; the minimum time for a degree is thus normally three years and the maximum can be six (or even more) years.

5. No formal requirements are needed for admission. Thus theoretically a person who has never gone into school can join a course, if he thinks he can benefit from it. He must, however, be 21 years or more of age. The age requirement was possibly imposed to discourage shift of students from conventional universities to the Open University. However, there is a persistent demand for age of admission to be reduced to 18.

6. Admissions are made on the "first come first served" basis except for the fact that quotas are prescribed for each region and for each category of applicants.

7. Each student receives 34 or 36 study units. Each unit is of about 48 pages and is likely to take a minimum of 10 hours. There is a considerable amount of exposition illustrated by diagrams and pictures wherever necessary. There are self-assessment exercises. There are also assignments which are marked either by a course instructor or are specially designed to be assessed by a computer. These marks obtained in these assignments together with marks of one final examination, held in November each year, are used to grade the student.

8. In science and technology courses, students are sent home-experiments kits containing chemicals, glassware, a specially-designed microscope, a calorimeter, a noisemeter, a binary computing device, a cathode-ray oscilloscope, etc.

9. Students spend 10% of their time on TV and radio programmes which are meant to supplement the written

The Open University

materials sent to the students. In some cases these are closely integrated with the course work, while in other cases, these are of the enrichment type.

10. In the summer, there are one-week residential schools which all foundation course students are required to attend. Some higher level courses also have summer school components. At these schools, it has been found that the students are highly motivated and the teachers who are recruited on part-time basis from the conventional universities enjoy teaching these students.

11. The University has 13 regional offices with responsibilites for the organisation of the important tutorial and counsellling services. There are also 300 study centres throughout the UK, located in existing educational institutions. These are open in the evenings and at week-ends and here students can receive face-to-face tuition, assistance and advice from tutors and counsellors and here they can also meet their fellow students. Most study-centres have TV computer terminals for mathematics lessons. The use of study centres is entirely optional for students. The university system is designed for home-based study.

12. In the first year 43,000 applications for 25,000 student places were received. In 1972, 20,500 were offered places out of 35,000 who had applied and for 1973, 17,500 were offered places out of 32,000 who had applied. Thus the total student population is more than 40,000 which makes it the largest university in UK.

13. The total annual budget of the Open University is about 10 million pounds, of which 80% is received directly from the government and the remaining 20% is received indirectly through the student fees which are again indirectly provided by the government through local authorities. This means an expenditure of about £ 250 per year per student which is cheaper as compared with £ 800 per year in conventional universities.

14. In November 1971, of the 19,000 registered students, 15,800 sat in the examination and 92·5% of these were successful in gaining a credit. Over 1,600 students were awarded no credits. Thus the overall percentage of success was about 75, which was considered quite satisfactory.

15. The University has established an educational technology unit. It gets feed-back from its students and analyses it. The University is also earning good royalties from the sale of its books.

16. The University has a staff of 1,100 full-time persons and has 4,000 tutors. There are training classes for tutors and the results of marking of assignment by the tutors are carefully moderated and normalised.

17. A careful analysis is made of the category of persons who apply and benefit from the courses, about 1/3rd are found to be teachers who immediately benefit from the programmes.

18. The fee for a foundation course consists of an initial payment of £ 10, a later payment of £ 15 and £ 25 for the summer school.

19. The Open University post-experience courses are meant for people in all kinds of employment who can benefit from further education but who cannot be released from their work to take conventional courses. Six such courses have been designed so far. These are :

(a) **Biological basis of behaviour** with 17 correspondence units, 17 TV programmes, 10 radio programmes, 8 computer-based assignments, 4 tutor-marked assignments, home experiment kit, one-week residential school and some Saturday sessions. The fee for this course is £ 80.

(b) **Computing and Computers.**
(c) **Electro-magnetics and Electronics.**
(d) **Reading Development.**
(e) **Reformation Studies.**
(f) **Background to School Mathematics.**

For each the student will not get a degree but will get a copy certificate or a letter of course completion.

20. The University has three higher degrees, namely, B. Phil, M. Phil and Ph.D. given on examination of a dissertation or a thesis submitted after successful completion of programmes of advanced study and research. For admission

into these post-graduate programmes, a person should have a good honours degree.

21. B. Phil. degree is intended for those who wish to undertake advanced study at post-graduate level in order to familiarise themselves with the method and techniques of research, or who wish to undertake a critical survey of the literature in a specific field of scholarship. The three research credits equivalent to 9 months' full-time study are required. For each credit, a satisfactory report from the supervisor is necessary.

22. The thesis for the M. Phil degree must show evidence of the candidate's proficiency in the methods and techniques of research, good style of presentation and adequate knowledge and discussion of the literature in a specific field. In must also show initiative, independence of thought and must be a distinct contribution to scholarship. Six research credits are required for this degree.

23. The thesis for the Ph.D. degree must show evidence of being a significant contribution to knowledge and of the capacity of the candidates to pursue further research without supervision and should be in a form suitable for publication. 9 research credits are required.

24. Comparison with correspondence courses conducted by the Indian universities show the following distinct features of the Open University :

(*a*) Radio and TV lessons are essential. (*b*) Study-centres work on week-ends throughout the country. (*c*) Different and more flexible course-structure than that of a conventional university. (*d*) Normal study of only one subject at time. (*e*) Some self-assessment exercises. (*f*) Development of new courses, new books and new TV and radio programmes. (*g*) Science kits for homes. (*h*) Science practicals during summer months. (*i*) Demonstration experiments on TV and discovery experiments at home. (*j*) Computer work in mathematics. (*k*) Courses specially designed for adults, more mature and better motivated students. (*l*) Honours degree by additional credits. (*m*) Provision of B. Phil. and M. Philand Ph.D. by theses with external supervision and students earning research credits at their convenience. (*n*) Post-experience courses. (*o*) Possibility of lifelong recurrent education. (*p*) Possibility of interchange of credits with conventional universities. (*q*) Greater development of educational techniques and use of mass media. (*r*) More intensive interdisciplinary courses. (*s*) Greater flexibility and possibility of taking courses from different faculties or the same faculty. (*t*) Only one such university in UK and the consequent economy of scale. (*u*) Publishing of its own newspaper 'Sesame' in which views of students and public are freely expressed. (*v*) No formal entry requirements for B.A. degree. (*w*) The possibility of developing 'hybrid' courses which will be formed by combining Open University and conventional university courses. (*x*) Innovation in every course. (*y*) A large organisational network throughout the country.

25. The Open University is open first as to people in as much as no formal academic qualification is required for registration. The Open University is also open as to methods. Every form of human communication is examined to see how it can be used to raise and broaden the level of human understanding. Finally the Open University is open also to ideas.

13

IMPLICATIONS OF MASS HIGHER EDUCATION FOR INDIA

1. A national conference on implications of mass higher education may be held soon to discuss the following questions :
   - (a) Can we plan for mass higher education by 1985 and have universal higher education by 2000 A.D. ?
   - (b) What sections of the society are under-represented in higer education and how can we encourage them to join the main stream of higher education ?
   - (c) What is the best compromise between excellence and egalitarianism in various universities ?
   - (d) Can we have an Open University with correspondence courses, TV, radio broadcasts, study centres, etc., with each major language as medium of instruction with its own programmes or should the correspondence courses and TV programmes be attached to existing universities ?
   - (e) Shall we have some excellent universities or shall our universities be of the same uniform standard, which with our limited resources cannot be very high ?
   - (f) How can we encourage the development of post-experience courses, both in private and public sectors ?

(g) What are the implications of Ashby's biological model in the Indian context?

(h) What are the results of studies of utilisation of buildings, libraries, laboratories, faculty time, other resources in our colleges and university departments?

(i) How can we provide for continuing education on a mass scale?

(j) In particular, what will be the best method of updating the knowledge of our school and college teachers?

(k) What have been the results of manpower planning so far and how more intensive manpower planning should be done in the near future?

(l) What are the relative costs of use of conventional lecture method, correspondence course method, open university method, use of video tapes, films and tape-recorders?

(m) What are the effects of labour market on trends in higher education?

(n) How can we strengthen higher education for ennobling and civilizing people?

(o) What role have students to play in higher education?

(p) What are the roles of the politicians and officials in higher education and how can their greater involvement be brought about in meaningful discussions on higher education?

(q) What can we learn from the experiences of developing and developed countries?

(r) What should be the role of research in higher education and in what proportion funds should be allotted to this research?

(s) How can we make higher education more relevant to the needs of the society?

(t) How can we make education more job-oriented and production-oriented?

(*u*) What changes in administrative structures of colleges and universities are needed to make them suitable instruments of change ?

(*v*) How to coordinate programmes of higher education when different languages are going to be used as media of instruction ?

(*w*) What will be the best means of financing higher education ?

(*x*) How can we encourage innovation in our system ?

(*y*) What can be the right goals for higher education in India ?

(*z*) Shall we have higher education as the monopoly of the youth or bring a significant number of adults into it and how to reconcile the autonomy of the universities with the accountability to the public ?

2. The above questions are typical of those which have to be answered for the development of higher education in India. We shall need quantitative investigations through sample surveys, scientific analysis of data and statistical techniques and this would mean investment of funds and scientific manpower in research in higher education.

3. There are many other aspects of higher education which have been discussed by the Kothari Commission, by various Vice-Chancellors' conferences in States and by the Inter-University Board conferences, etc. It is obvious that the problems are so varied, so complex and so important that many conferences may be required. These conferences will not arrive at decisions but will provoke thinking and generate many series of investigations based on sound principles of social science research.

4. Each of these conferences should be preceded by 1 to 2 years of hard preparatory work. The UGC should support these conferences on a generous scale.

5. India should also take the initiative in holding conferences in higher education for developing countries with the support from UNESCO and the concerned countries. The Lancaster conference was mainly for developed countries.

Since developing countries have their own problems, it may be good for them to get together and find common solutions to the problems of higher education.

6. There should be one or more centres of higher education in India. Many of our education departments in universities concentrate on school education. Some of these should concentrate on higher education and further education. The universities undertake research on social, scientific and technological problems of other sections of society. They should do some research on their own problems also.

7. Our economists should take a great interest in economics of higher education. When vast resources are being made available, thinking on their optimum utilisation is very vital.

8. Students, government officials and political decision-makers should be encouraged to participate in all such discussions in a significant and not just a token manner. They should feel really involved.

9. We should have more journals devoted to higher education in our country. There should be public debates on all important national issues of higher education.

10. India should be adequately represented in all international conferences on higher education so that our achievements and innovations can be highlighted in these conferences and we can also learn from the current experiences of other countries.

11. Comparative higher education should be a serious subject of study and research in some universities.

12. The possibility of our using TV channels in different cities, closed circuit TV and satellite transmission TV should be fully explored.

14

EDUCATION AND RESEARCH ACTIVITIES IN ADELAIDE

1. **Introduction**

The account in this and the following four chapters, of higher education, continuing education and research in Australia is based on the author's visit to that country at the invitation of the Australian Vice-Chancellors' Committee. Eleven of the fifteen universities in Australia were visited and discussions on higher education were held with vice-chancellors, registrars, professors, scientists, educationists, government officials and students in Adelaide, Canberra, Melbourne, Sydney, Newcastle, Townsville and Brisbane. These cities have about 75% of total Australian population and more than 75% of educational and research activities in Australia are located in these cities. Chapters 14—17 give a detailed account of these activities while Chapter 18 contains a comparative study of educational systems of India and Australia.

2. **University of Adelaide**

The Council of the university (Corresponding to Executive Council or Syndicate in our universities) has the following as members : chancellor, vice-chancellor, five members elected by Parliament, eight members elected by academic faculty, twelve persons elected by graduates and others who are not employees of the university, one postgraduate student and four undergraduate students.

Corresponding to our Academic Council, the university has an Education Committee which is supreme in academic matters and has 10% members as students' representatives. The university has the following committees : Finance Committee, Planning Committee, Allocations Committee, Staff Development Committee, Equipment Committee, Research Committee, Computer Centre Committee, Industrial Liaison Committee, Public Relations Committee, Publications Committee, Study Leave Committee, Sports Committee, Discipline Board, Library Committee, Adult Education Board, Appointments Board, Committee on outside Grants for Research and so on. It has faculties of Agriculture, Architecture and town planning, Arts, Dentistry, Economics, Engineering, Law, Mathematical Sciences, Medicine, Music, Science, Technology and Applied Sciences. Students are represented on all faculties and on some of the Committees. The central administration has the Vice-Chancellor's office, Registrar's office with the Staff unit, Architectural unit, Administration of General services unit, Academic Registrar's office, Bursar's Office, Computer Centre, Health Services, University Union, Students' Representation Council, Adult Education Unit, etc.

After 12 years of school which consists of 5 years of primary education and 7 years of secondary education (in some other states it is 6 plus 6), a student joins the university for a three years' bachelor's degree and one year's honours degree. There are institutes of technology which give three years' diploma courses in technology as against three and four years' degree courses in the university. These are now being upgraded to advanced colleges of education and will give both the degree and diploma and make available bridging over courses also.

A student has to pay about 600 dollars per year as fees and the government spends on him an average of about 1,500-2,000 dollars, so that the total expenditure per student per annum comes to about Rs. 20,000 to 25,000 per year as compared to corresponding expenditure of about Rs. 600 to 1,000 in India.

3. Adult Education, Further Education and Radio University

The department of Adult Education of the University of Adelaide runs courses for adults such as the Modern Short Story, Australian Literary Scene, Modern Indian Fiction, Art and Aesthetics, Geo-morphology of South Australia, Pollution of Water, Land and Air in S. A., Marine and Fresh Water Fishes of S. A., Birds of S. A., Australian Oceanography, Philosophy at work, Child Psychology, Child Care and Development, Mass Media, Politics in S.A., Industrial Democracy, Preparation for retirement, Foreign Languages (French, German, Russian, Chinese, Japanese, Indonesian, Malaysian, etc.).

Radio University runs courses such as the following : You and Your Child, Specific Learning Difficulties, Writer as a Social Critic, Negro Literature, Economic Issues in Asia, Accountancy for other Professions, Colour Television, New Developments in Pharmacy, Africa Today, Ecology and the Family, Science Fiction, Literature for Children, Restless Earth, Fiscal Policies, Noise in the Community.

One course by the department every year is run in the countryside where about 60 or 70 families come in their cars with their camps and classes are arranged on Nature Study, Conservation and Pollution for both the adults and children. A new course on River Pollution is run for one week in the countryside and for one week on a boat in a river where field studies are made. The lectures are written by the Faculty of the university and even by men in public life and fees from students usually meet the cost. Minimum enrolment has to be 12 and the maximum can be 60. Courses on Orthonology, Geology, Flowers, Fishes are popular, while courses on Basic Physics, Basic Chemistry, etc., are not. A course for elementary school teachers given by Dienes was popular, but a course on secondary mathematics arranged by Australian Association of Mathematics Teachers was not. Fees are high for courses for Businessmen and Engineers and low for other courses.

The department co-operates in the organisation of a Writers' Week once in three years where writers from Australia and other countries come and discuss.

The Radio works for three to four hours each day, for four days in a week. The difficulty is about shortage of persons, who can produce the programmes. The Radio covers a population of 100 thousand persons.

The State department of Further Education provides more than 1,000 part-time evening courses mostly of a technical nature for a total of 80,000 in-service people every year. Classes are held in the evenings in technical colleges and buildings and equipments of the schools are used. The department was formerly a part of the department of technical education, but as a result of the report of the Committee for re-organization of education in S.A., it has now been separated.

The courses cover a wide variety. For example, some typical courses are the following :—

Technicians Certificates (Automotive, Building, Commerce, Electronics, Industrial, Mechanical, Personnel, Photography, Public services) ; *Post-trade Certificates* (Electric fitter, Furniture trade, Metal fabrication, Motor mechanic, Motor painter, Motor body drawing, Decoration, Plumbing, Refrigeration mechanic) ; *Other Certificates* (Banking, Agriculture, Child care, Commercial Art, Craft, Valuers, Dress making, Hardware sales, Horticulture, Industrial Relations, Insurance, Instrument mechanics, Local government clerks, Local government overseers, Land brokers, Meat inspection, Occupational safety, Plumbing, Radio and TV, Stenography, Supervision, Transport administration); *General Adult Classes* (Art advertisement, Art appreciation, Creative design, China painting, Floral art, Graphic arts, Ikabana Life drawing, Painting, Pencil sketching, Water-colour technique, Book keeping, Business principles, Typewriting, Shorthand, Motor maintenance, Asian and European cooking, Basket making, Batiks, Blacksmithing, Bookbinding, Copper and silver crafts, Crochet, French flower making, Glass blowing, Knitting, Landscaping, Jewellery, Lampshades making, Mosaics, Pottery, Rug making, Sculpture, Toy making, Upholstery, Weaving and spinning, Welding, Dance and drama appreciation, Dress making, Electronics, Engineering, English, Gardening, Geology, Languages, Mathematics, Metal works, Music of all types, Navigation, Philosophy, Photography, Wood-works, Physical Culture, Computer mechanics, Biology, Philately, Librarianship); *Vocational subjects* (Agriculture, Automotive, Buildings, Business and Commerce, Electronic, Graphic arts, Plumbing, Sheet metal works, Textiles) and courses for matriculation students.

Some of the courses are for three years—one hour per week or 40 hours a year on a block time basis. There are adult matriculation courses where an adult can appear in matriculation examination in two stages of 2+3 years. Sandwich courses are also available.

The government has declared its policy of making all tertiary education free and this may influence enrolment in part-time courses.

4. Teaching and Research in Computer Science

The department of computer science is part of the faculty of Mathematical Sciences and is separate from the Computer Centre. It offers B.Sc. and B.Sc. (Honours) degrees and certificate, diploma and short-term courses in programming. In the third Year of B.Sc., students take courses in computer system, numerical analysis, assembling languages, data structure, graphs and systems response, programming languages, etc. The diploma is a full-time one year or part-time two years' course and consists in training in numerical analysis, computer systems, programming, data structure, data management and a project. For the honours courses, a student has to select a topic from the following : logical design of computer systems, operating systems, advanced numerical analysis, information theory, operations research, advanced programming languages, theory of languages, computer architecture, computer networks. They have also to do a major computing project each.

Work on validation of simulation models and on interaction of computers languages with formalistic and structural approaches to linguistics is also being done.

5. Scientific organisations

The Australian Academy of Sciences corresponds to the Indian National Science Academy. It has 163 Fellows and elects 9 Fellows every year. It published an adaptation of

Biological School Study Group text-book of USA and this book was adopted as a text-book all over the country giving a large amount of royalty income to the Academy which it proposes to invest in improvement of science and mathematics education. The Academy is also going to collaborate with the two other learned Academies, namely, Australian Academy of Social Sciences and Australian Academy of Humanities in a joint environmental project called the "Botany Bay Project" which is financially supported by the Commonwealth Government.

The Australian and New Zealand Association for the Advancement of Science (ANZAAS) corresponds to our Indian Science Congress Association. It held its 45th session in Perth when I was in Australia. It has, however, a wider coverage and has 31 sections including sections on architecture and town planning, pharmaceutical sciences, optometry, agriculture and forestry, micro-biology, physiology, veterinary science, geographical sciences, education, economics, industrial relations, anthropology, history and sociology.

One interesting section of ANZAAS is STUDENT ANZAAS where popular lectures for students are given. Students can however also attend other symposia and lectures in other sections. In 1973 the following series of lectures were arranged in Student Anzaas :

The origin of life on earth (A planet is born, origin of life, microbes to man, the balance in nature).

The future of life on earth (population growth through time, distribution of malnutrition and disease, waste and recycling as for example in spaceship, responsibilities of those with knowledge);

Genetic engineering (DNA & RNA protein, genetic code, experimental genetic manipulation, viruses, cells, bacteria, ethics of gene manipulation, human potential);

Computer and information retrieval (history and development of computers in science, medicine and agriculture, ethical issues of information control ;

The role of Science.

The theme of that year's ANZAAS conference was

'Science, Development and Environment' and a large number of well-planned symposia were organised on subjects like the following : Economic growth, a magnificent obsession ? ; The Clash of value systems; The scientists, the bureaucrats and the environmental responsibility; limits to growth in Australia; Is it too late for Western Australia to secede ? The implications of nuclear explosions; Resources management and planning, ideals and reality; The Australian aboriginals, the widening gap; Education and environment; Whither urban Australia ?; Social problems of development, Science and manpower planning.

In the mathematical sciences section, there were symposia on simulation, quantitative methods in mining and exploration and teaching mathematics to non-mathematicians. There were also papers in general mathematics dealing with physical oceanography, operations research, fishing, pest control, farm management, thermal pollution etc. The programme reflects the importance given to relevance in mathematical sciences research.

6. Flinders University of South Australia

When enrolments in the University of Adelaide reached about 7,000, the university started a campus away from the town which in 1966 developed into the modern Flinders University. It has a fine site overlooking the town and the sea and commands a magnificent view at night. The university has started the schools of physical, mathematical, biological and social sciences and humanities rather than with the traditional departments. The architecture is most modern and has provided for even an artificial lake. New inter-disciplinary programmes and innovative ideas are being tried in this university.

15

EDUCATION AND RESEARCH ACTIVITIES IN CANBERRA

1. Australian National University

The ANU was created by an act of Commonwealth (Australian) Parliament in 1946. In September 1960, the Canberra University college was incorporated and since that time the University has operated academically into two distinct but inter-related parts, namely, the Institute of Advanced Studies (IAS) and the School of General Studies (SGS). The SGS functions as a teaching university and has more than 4,000 undergraduate students and more than 500 students working for masters and Ph.D. Degrees. It carries out both undergraduate and postgraduate training and original research. It has the following faculties :

(*i*) Faculty of Arts : (Applied mathematics ; Classics; English, French, Geography; German, History, Linguistics, Medieval Studies, Philosophy, Political Science, Pre-history and Anthropology, Pure mathematics, Russian, Sociology).

(*ii*) Faculty of Asian Studies : (Asian Civilization, Chinese, Indonesian, Japanese, South Asian and Buddhist).

(*iii*) Faculty of Economics : (Accounting and Public Finance, Administrative Studies, Computer Science, Econometrics, History, Economics, Mathematical Statistics).

(*iv*) Faculty of Law.

(*v*) Faculty of Science : (Bio-Chemistry, Botany, Chemistry, Geology, Physics, Psychology, Theoretical Physics, Zoology).

The IAS which is a centre for Research and for training for Research consists of the following Schools :

(*i*) School of Medical Research : (Bio-Chemistry, Clinical Science, Experimental Pathology, Human Biology, Immunology, Medical Chemistry, Microbiology, Physical Bio-Chemistry, Physiology).

(*ii*) Research School of Physical Sciences : (Applied Mathematics, Astronomy, Engineering, Physics, Geophysics, Solid State Physics, Theoretical Physics, Diffusion).

(*iii*) Research School of Social Sciences : (Demography, Economic History, Economics, History, Law, Philosophy, Political Science, Sociology, Statistics, Education Research Unit, History of Ideas Unit, Urban Research Unit, Australian Dictionary of Biography).

(*iv*) Research School of Pacific Studies : (Anthropology and Sociology. Biogeography and Geomorphology, Economics, Far Eastern History, Human Geography, International Relations, Linguistics, Pacific History, Pre-History, New Guinea Research Unit, Strategic and Defence Study Centre, Contemporary Research Centre).

(*v*) Research School of Chemistry : (Inorganic, Organic, Physical, Theoretical, Physical, Organic).

(*vi*) Research School of Biological Science : (Developmental Biology, Environmental Biology, Genetics, Neurobiology, Population Biology, Molecular Biology, Taxonomy).

(*vii*) School of Earth Sciences : (Geophysics, Geochemistry, Geo Fluid Dynamics).

There is also a hundred inch Anglo-Australian Telescope for penetrating 1,000 million light years into the Southern skies.

Besides the directors and deans, the permanent academic staff of the Institute comprises professors, readers, professorial fellows, senior fellows, and fellows. In addition to permanent staff, senior fellows are appointed for a period of two to five years. The Institute has about 500 members on the academic staff and about 350 full-time research students, all of whom get scholarships. Besides, a large number of foreign scientists come to spend their sabbatical leave at the Institute. Faculty members get their sabbatical leave for one in four years and during this period they get their full salary and some allowance for expenses.* The principal responsibility of every member is to do research and advance knowledge and he has no other duties except guiding students and being of help to other universities and the government. In SGS there are about 350 faculty members and 4,700 students giving a student-stuff ratio of about 13.51. The University library has 6 lakh books but is decentralised for effective use. The Computer Centre has a Univac 1108, an IBM 360/50 and a PDP 11/45.

The University is governed by a Council which has similar powers as our Executive Council and has one representative of each of undergraduate, postgraduate and research students. Corresponding to our Court, it has a Convocation consisting of old graduates and other distinguished members. Instead of the Academic Council, it has Academic Boards of IAS and SGS.

The Vice-Chancellor is the principal executive officer of the university. The Deputy Vice-Chancellor helps him in matters of academic policy, while the Secretary to the university helps in financial matters and in supervision of university administration. The Registrar is the secretary of the Council and of the Boards. The Bursar is responsible for budgets and accounts and the Academic Registrar looks after both the IAS and SGS.

On 30th April 1971, the University had 327 teaching staff, 572 research staff, 550 technical staff, 130 library staff, 77 central staff, 387 central administrative staff, 203 departmental administrative staff, 30 construction staff, and 522 maintenance and others making a total of 2,284 employees. It has 546 Ph.D. students, 187 M.Sc. students, 3,857 B.Sc. students, 230 non-degree students, making a total of about 4,804 students, giving a ratio of 1.7 employees for every student. Out of 4,804 students, 2,485 received financial assistance from the university or the government.

For the year ending 30th December 1971, the income was about 28 crores of rupees from the Government and about 1 crore of rupees from the fees. Expenditure was Rs. 12 crores on IAS, Rs. 6 crores on SGS, Rs. 2 crores on Library, Rs. 1.4 crores on administration and the rest on miscellaneous items. Expenditure per student came to more than Rs. 60,000 per year, though only 40% of the amount could be accounted towards teaching.

The IAS is similar to our Tata Institute of Fundamental Research, but it is within the University framework, has Ph.D. programme of its own and problems of research are chosen from the point of view of the needs of the country. Every year more than 150 scholars come and stay at the IAS for periods of one month to one year. The IAS has reversed the brain drain, because now people from other countries come to Australia. It has established high international reputation and gives full facilities to faculty members from other Australian universities to spend their time here. The IAS appears to be an exciting place for people to work and the ANU wants to keep it as such.

2. **The University Centre for Resources and Environmental Studies (CRES)**

It is a non-departmental multi-disciplinary centre embracing natural and social sciences and humanities, intending to use brains, typewriters and computers, with one professor of system analysis and one professor of resources economics and others. It has the formidable task of making an inventory of Australian resources, both renewable and non-renewable, to ensure that these resources can be developed in the general interest of all Australians. It will work in close collaboration with the CSIRO, the three learned Academies and other environment projects in other universities. The three projects at present are : (*i*) the preparation of the Inventory of the resources, (*ii*) planning of land use in relation to recreation and leisure and (*iii*) the urban environmental problems. CRES intends to undertake masters and Ph.D. programmes also.

3. Human resources programme

This programme aims to be multi-disciplinary and to try to take a wholistic view of man. The first year unit on Human Biology provides an introduction to first principles. Human Ecology unit examines man's evolution and his influence on the environment. The third unit will be on Human Adaptability and will focus on evolving adaptability of human beings, at both individual and social levels to changing conditions of life. Thus Human Sciences will be one of the subjects in the undergraduate programme. This course will meet a genuine demand of students.

4. Canberra Technical College

This College has about 9,000 students of which less than 1,000 are full time. Others come for one night (3 hours) a week or two nights a week. According to law in Australia, every tradesman has to receive training for one day (8 hours) a week for 30 weeks for 3 years' equivalent time, and the employer has to give him leave for this period. Thus every tradesman works for 4 days in a week in the trade and learns for one day in the college and he gets two days' rest in a week.

The Department of Technical Education of New South Wales conducts about 700 courses providing training for 70,000 students of all ages and interests, in 61 colleges, of which CTC is one.

The Certificate courses are on a four-year part-time basis requiring from 3 to 12 hours' attendance each week. Certificate courses give instruction of a more advanced nature in specialised fields. Trades courses are meant for apprentices engaged in skilled trades and most of these are of 3 years' duration on one full day per week basis. Post-trade courses are for further training and updating of training of tradesmen. There are also specialised courses.

This college has the following Schools :

Applied Electricity, Art, Automotive, Biology, Building, Commerce, Electrical Engineering, Fashion, Food, General Studies, Graphic Arts, Hair Dressing, Home Science, Management, Mechanical and Civil Engineering, Mechanical Engineering

Trades, Navigation, Plumbing and Sheet Metal, Rural Studies, Secretarial Studies, Vehicle Trades.

Some typical courses are listed below :

Applied Electricity : (Electric fitter, mechanics, Office machine mechanics, radio, refrigeration mechanics, industrial electronics, TV receiving sets, Electrical wiring).

Biological Sciences : (Biology research techniques, animal care, community service).

Building : (draftsman, carpentry and joining, carpet weaving, painting and decorating, sign writing, silks painting, colour planning, scaffolding, concrete practice, critical path programme).

Fashion : (Clothes construction techniques, garment assembling, pattern making, house furnishing, textile appreciation, fashion appreciation, needle work).

Food : (hotel and catering management, butchery, commercial cooking, wine service).

Graphic Arts : (photography, book-binding, machine composing, layout and designing, photo composing, lithography).

Home Science : (general cookery, advanced cookery, cake decorating, buffet dishes, desserts, international cooking, oriental cooking, Chinese cooking).

Rural Studies : (horticulture, sheep and wool, pastures and crops, wild flowers, floral arts, home gardening).

Secretarial Practices : (stenography, typing, office management).

Some courses are popular with housewives who come for years together for one night a week. I visited fashion, secretarial practices, home science, hair dressing and plumbing departments and found the latest equipment there.

When a number of persons desire a course, it is started if at least 12 persons are willing to join and there is likely to be this much demand in future. In addition to full-time teachers, the college has also a large number of part-time teachers from industry and business. The college is constantly on the lookout for the needs of the community assessing these needs and providing for them through courses in different technical colleges according to the needs of the communities they serve.

5. Canberra College of Advanced Education

Australia has 15 universities with about 1,30,000 students. Three more Universites are going to start functioning from January 1975. Besides, there are also about 80 Institutes of Technology and Colleges of Advanced Education which have an additional 80,000 students in tertiary education. CCAE is one of the largest and best of these with about 3,000 students about 2,000 of whom study for 3 years' degree and 1,000 of whom are graduates who study one-year diploma course in computing, teaching, library science, administrative studies, etc. It is an autonomous institution giving its own diplomas and degrees. At present it has the following schools :

(i) School of Administrative Studies (ii) School of Applied Sciences (iii) School of Information Sciences (iv) School of Liberal Studies (v) School of Teacher Education (vi) School of Environmental Education.

It also intends to start a School of Para Medical Studies in response to the needs of the community. Management law, Languages (Russian, German, Chinese, Japanese), Library Science, Computer Science, Geology, Journalism, Professional Writing, Teacher Education, Secretarial Practices are all parts of Undergraduate Programme. The following are the courses offered :

Finite Mathematics, Computers and Computing, Micro-Economics I-II, Administration I-III, Concepts of Elements of Law; Macro-Economics I-II, Administrative Law, Statistical Investigations, Urban Economics, Urban Planning, Accounting I-II, Management Accounts, Financial Accounts, Financial Management, Auditing Accounting Systems, Probability, Government Accounts, Sample Survey designs, Experimental Designs, Monetary Economics, International Economics, Public Finance, Managerial Economics, Labour Economics, Professional Writing I-VI, Contemporary English Language I-VI, Uses of Spoken English, Basic Mathematical Techniques, Analytical Geometry and Topology, Calculus I-II, Algebraic Structures, LinearAlgebraic & Differential equations I-II, Numerical Analysis I-V, Combinatorial Mathematics I-II, Mathematics of Operations Research, Control Theory, Boolean Algebraic Systems, Human Geography, Resources Location, Mapping, Cartography I-II, Air Photo Interpretation, Physical Environment, Geography of South East Asia, Russian I-VI, Spoken Chinese I-VI, Written Chinese I-VI, Japanese I-VI, Executive Stenography I-II, Business Communications, Law and Procedure of Meetings, Libraries and Education, International Library Resources, Resources for Information and Research, Cataloguing and Classification, Library for children, Animal Biology I-II, Plant Biology I-II, Organic Chemistry, Biological Chemistry, Basic Surface Geology, Microphysics and Electricity, Waves, Protons and Electrons, Genetics, Ecology, Inorganic Chemistry, Applied Physical Chemistry, Organic Chemistry, Biochemistry I-II, Applied Geo-Chemistry, Mineralogy and Petrology, Stratigaphy and Sedimentation, Fluid Geology and Photogeology, Electro Magnetism, Quantum and Atomic Physics, Electronics I-IV, Wild Life Biology and Management, Plant Growth, Fish Biology and Management, Ecological conservation of resources, Land Uses and Resources Management, Recreational Planning and Management, Park Administration, Biophysical Chemistry, Economic Geology, Engineering Geology, Hydrology, Solid State Physics, Applied Geophysics, Analysis of information, Bibliographical and reference services, Organisation of Library materials, the Educational Role of the Library, Comparative Librarianship, Business procedure, Office Administration, Executive Secretarial Practice; Information Systems I-IV, Computer Programme I-IV, Computer Organisation I-IV, Computation Methods I-III, Basic Issues of Education, Foundations of Education, History of Mathematical Thought, Complex Variable theory, Calculus of Variations, Optimisation, History I-IX, Surveying, Land Tenure and Settlement, Location Analysis, Quantitative Geography, Geography of Organisations, Social Geography, Office Management, Administrative Organization, Applied Microscopy, Population Ecology, Basic Physical Management, Commercial Law I-II, Business Management, Inference and decision-making, Economics in Industry, Economics in Development, School Libraries, Historical Bibliography, Children Literature, Educational Materials Centres, Journalism I-IV, Literary Studies I-VIII, Advanced Microphysics and Thermodynamics, Industrial Chemistry, Teaching-Learning Processes, Curriculum Study, Practice of Teaching I-II, Child and School, School and Society; Aims of Teaching, English Expression, Curricular design, Educational Studies I-VIII, Art, Shorthand for Journalists I-II, Operations Research Techniques, Forecasting and Time-series; Regression and Multivariate Analysis, Environmental and Population Chemistry, Geological Investigations, Advanced Report Writing, Human Ecology, Structural Geology, Development Administration, Australian Government Politics I-II, Malaysian Politics, Indian Politics, International Politics I-II, General Chemistry, Basic Mathematical Chemistry, Music I-IV, Education and Development, Programming Techniques I-II, Systems Analysis I-II, Simulation Techniques, Linear Optimisation, Administration I-VIII, Applied Plant Pathology. Ecological Geology, Soil Sciences, Constitutional Law.

Some features of the colleges of Advanced Education are: (*a*) applied bias, (*b*) needs of the community in view, (*c*) all emphasis on teaching and relatively little on research, (*d*) teachers with industrial and public administrative experience preferred to those with research experience only, (*e*) use of educational technology on a large scale and (*f*) part-time students.

There is however competition for government funds between colleges of advanced education and universities and the results are yet to be seen.

The following extracts from the third report (1973-1975) of the Australian Commission on Advanced Education are relevant.

(*i*) We have been impressed with the way in which old and familiar educational administrative problems are being tackled in new and varied ways. There is a general willingness to abandon hide-bound or traditional attitudes and to experiment in such vital matters as student selection techniques, the use of educational technology in teaching programmes and in design of interdisciplinary curricula to meet the needs of the community.

(*ii*) It is encouraging to observe that the changes taking place within the colleges are being duly noted by the community at large. There is awakening public interest in the opportunity being created by the existence of the colleges—opportunities for industry and various commercial groups as well as for intending students. Increasingly the courses offered in colleges are accepted as having the necessary validity and making their special contribution to tertiary education.

(*iii*) We fully believe that the hopes and aspirations which were entertained by those who originally encourged Commonwealth participation in this field of tertiary Education have been justified both by the developments which have taken place as also by those which are now being planned to be introduced.

(*iv*) The basic purpose of the colleges is to increase the range of opportunity for tertiary education. The Commission is concerned to note the signs that the original aim is tending to change by academic pressures. The temptation to follow certain overseas institutions along the path of 'academic respectability' gives rise to many tensions. We urge college authorities to adhere steadfastly to the declared aims.

(*v*) If colleges should ever emphasise research at the expense of undergraduate teaching or concentrate on full-time students to the exclusion of part-time students or give priority to degree courses while diploma courses are allowed to languish or accept students and appoint staff solely on the grounds that they have acquired traditional academic qualifications or divert their attention from the technological and social needs of the community, the college system would have failed.

Some of the advanced colleges specialise in instruction, for example, agricultural colleges or schools, conservatia of Music, schools of physiotherapy and colleges offering courses in advanced nursing administration; domestic science, forestry, horticultural science and occupational therapy. The emphasis on all courses is on practical applications of the knowledge and close contact with the primary and manufacturing industries, commerce, government and community services. The courses provide orientation to technology-based professions and other professions such as accountancy, teaching, art, music and agriculture. The educational programmes are designed to produce practitioners who are able to adapt themselves to changes arising from rapid progress in the technological field.

Each course in a college has to be approved by the department, by the school, by the college council, by the course advisory committee consisting of members of the public and prospective employers, by the assessors appointed by the government and finally by the education minister.

In recruitment of staff, experience in industry is desirable. Very often this factor does not influence faculty recruitment in universities. The number of students in colleges of advanced education in 1973 is 63,000 and is expected to go to 81,000 in 1975.

6. Australian Vice-Chancellors' Committee

This committee consists of Vice-Chancellors of all Universities (including one in Griffeths, one in Murdoch and one in Wallingong, all of which will start functioning in 1975) and meets five times in a year in alternate months. In the intervening months, only the executive committee meets to dispose of routine-matters. This is unlike our Inter-University Board of India where all Vice-Chancellors meet once a year and the standing committee meets four times in a year. Each meeting takes place at two informal dinners and a formal full-day meeting. The Committee worked like a Vice-Chancellors' Club from 1920 till about 1960. However, now its advice is seriously considered both by the government as well as by the Australian University Commission. Each University makes a contribution to the committee as a certain percentage of its budget and the AVCC meets expenses on travel by the Vice-Chancellors. The Committee has emphasised educational research and co-ordinates activities for improvement of teaching. It holds regular conferences and workshops on teaching methods and the Australian Universities Commission gives special funds for the same. The AVCC is also the agency for implementing Australian-Asian Universities Co-operation Scheme on which the Commonwealth government spends about 250,000 dollars per year. The main project under the scheme has been that of cooperation with Indonesia in the fields of agricultural production and includes grants for library equipment, books and technical journals published in Australia, for visits of administrators and senior academics to Indonesia, organization of short courses of lectures there, awarding of fellowships for postgraduate training in Australia and provision of stop-overs by Australian professors when visiting other countries.

The main functions of the AVCC were spelt out in 1968 as follows :

(*i*) to provide a forum whereby universities can take counsel together in matters of mutual interest, (*ii*) to formulate advice to university bodies, (*iii*) to make public pronouncements or take other appropriate actions whenever it believes this can be useful, (*iv*) to collect and disseminate to the universities information on matters of mutual interest and concern.

The AVCC has cooperated closely with AUC (Australian Universities Commission), DES (Department of Education and Science), CACAE (Commonwealth Advisory Committee on Advanced Education), ARGC (Australian Research Grants Committee), CSIRO (Commonwealth Scientific and Industrial Research Organisation), FAUSA (Federation of Australian Universities Staff Association), NUAUS (National Union of Australian Universities Students) and has presented university views on all important matters.

The AVCC has organised conferences on Higher Education, Conferences of Chairmen of Professorial Boards and Conferences of University Registrars. It has served as a house for information on all matters and has underwritten the Journal 'The Australian University'.

The following remarks from the report of the chairman of the AVCC are of some interest :

(*i*) Persons with Ph.D. training are not only the source of university teachers, but are also required by government research institutions and by industry on an increasing scale. During this training, a student learns how to marshall a considerable amount of information which he has already acquired, to think clearly, to plan the attack upon a problem and in general to use the tools with which he has been equipped. It is during this period that the better class graduate acquires the confidence, skill and expertise which fits him for leadership in life. Another aspect of research in the university is the contribution which it makes to the efficiency of the general teaching in the universities.

(*ii*) Post-graduate students engaged in research in university receive on the whole less money than they would if they were employed in government department and in industry and in similar work and in compensation for this they receive training and a higher degree. The diversity of research interests in a large university makes it possible for expensive equipment to be used by a wider range of people and for a wider range of purposes than would be the case in a moderate-sized government research organisation or in an industrial research laboratory. Again, because of diversity of interests in the university, the probability of new ideas developing from cross-fertilisation in inter-disciplinary areas is far greater than is the case in the division of a government institute which is largely concerned with a single objective.

(*iii*) At a later stage, the universities may be expected to concentrate further on scholarship and fundamental research. The colleges of advanced education remain oriented towards the application to the more immediate needs of the country through technological and vocational courses though these invariably include a liberal element. Each will therefore appeal to a different group of students. Most students entering college will have selected beforehand the profession they wish to enter. Many university students, particularly in arts and social sciences, will not have done so. College students will normally pass immediately into employment in industry, while university student may proceed to research. Admission requirements for both should be flexible but for college admission, greater weight should be given to experience in industry and to the degree of maturity. The major consideration must be the prospect of success in the course attempted.

(*iv*) Universities and colleges have different functions in research. The universities, but not the colleges, have a responsibility to pursue knowledge for its own sake. The colleges have an important role to play in shorter-term research and investigations closely related to the needs of industry and much of it will be supported by the industry itself. Some of this research will demand knowledge and skills of a very high order, but it is not intended that the college should offer courses leading to higher research degree. Educational research should, however, be encouraged both in colleges and universities.

(*v*) In 1970 NUAUS decided to seek an end to academic tenure which it claimed protected the incompetent and uninterested university teachers. However, later it changed its stand to demand the following instead :

- (*a*) establishment of teaching and learning units within universities;
- (*b*) all university teachers, particularly newly appointed ones, should be required to attend courses given by these units;
- (*c*) teaching ability should be taken into account in making appointments and in determining promotions.

(*vi*) The AVCC is united in its view that the universities will be greatly harmed if they are used as a vehicle for promoting political views. The prime purposes of universities everywhere are scholarship and enhancing the education of students of all ages and discovery and creation of new knowledge and these purposes are jeopardised when universities are used as pressure points.

(*vii*) While in Australia, commerce and industry have been generous to the universities, there is need for close cooperation between universities and major employers in industry, commerce and government, so that there is more understanding on both sides, of the aims and objects of university education in the modern world. A balance has to be struck between the educational and practical values of courses taught in universities.

(*viii*) When more than 80% of the capital and recurrent expenditure is provided from the public purse, the universities have to be accountable to the Government and the general public.

(*ix*) The AUC is charged on behalf of the government "with the task of promoting balanced development in universities so that the resources can be used to the greatest possible advantage of Australia." To meet this obligation, it can take steps which may harm university autonomy. This requires mutual understanding.

(*x*) The AVCC is not satisfied on the score of accountability. Universities must, for example, look at their teaching performance and the effectiveness of their use of other resources of manpower and equipment. The AVCC has a positive role to play here by giving leadership, by encouraging the study of problems facing the universities, by pooling resources for research into vital questions of admissions, teaching methods, course standards, examination techniques, by fostering cooperation with secondary schools, colleges of advanced education, teacher colleges and with government and by forging links with these and the AUC.

(*xi*) The greatest assurance of university autonomy and academic freedom is good performance. Should the universities fail to give a good account of themselves, they will clearly invite more direct intervention by government agencies than is necessary or sensible.

7. ANU Centre for Continuing Education

The Centre has close associations with adult education and university continuing education work in India, since all the three senior staff members, Dr. Duke, Mr. Crew and Dr Hains, have spent some time there. The Centre has the following activities :

(*i*) **Provision of carefully selected class programmes in evenings for residents of the city of Canberra,** with the assistance of faculty members of ANU and CAE. The courses and enrolment in 1972 were as follows :

Women in Australia (85), Chemistry of life (33), Society and drugs (30), Geology (76), High energy physics (16), Trees and forests (23), Meteorology and environmental resources (34), Pollution and ecology (25), Animal biology (25), Inter-relationships between science, technology and society (10), Geometric transformations (15), Statistical analysis (16), Digital computers (27), Computers and Society (11), Archaeology in Australia (25), Influence of Plato (41), Christianity (24), Hinduism (64), Buddhism (64), Islam (12), Civilizations of South East Asia (29), Australian History (37), Probability (28), Urban Geography (24), Modern Japan (39), Contemporary China (89), Modern Indonesia (58), Economic theory and practice (44), Industrial relations (28), Conscience, freedom and law (57), Contemporary legal problems (45), Design for living (27), Contemporary Novels (24), Australian art (28), Creative work (38), Poetry understanding (14), Mass Media (17), Sociology (32), Social Psychology (24), Learning through group experience (12), French, German, Spanish, Indonesian, Dutch, etc. (10-30).

(ii) **National Seminars and Conferences on issues of social, economic, political, scientific and educational concern through research conferences, small group conferences and encounters :** The Centre brings together academic people with perfect theories and decision-makers in various fields in critical situations needing urgent solutions in encounters or small-group conferences on the neutral grounds of the Centre for realistic discussions of problems and situations. A great deal of preparatory work goes into each of the conferences, wherein members of the Centre have discussions with various parties concerned, hold small conferences for building up agenda and finally hold a higher conference where papers are circulated and small groups or syndicates hold discussion informally and arrive at decisions. Such search conferences were held, for example, for the following topics :

Graduates for what ? Employment of sociology graduates, Education of resident medical officers and of nurses, On small group learning, On development of human resources, On trade relations with neighbouring countries. Although evaluation is still going on, these conferences appear to be successful.

(iii) **Refresher courses and summer schools for professional and occupational groups** : These were of larger duration and were organised for the following topics :

Religion (Conscience in the Seventies).

Journalism (Press, Parliament and Privilege).

Restrictive trade practices.
Intensive language courses.
Mathematics for social scientists.
Pharmacy refresher course.
Health and welfare in-service training courses.

(*iv*) **Research in continuing education** : There is need for research in both theoretical and empirical aspects in this field and for starting post-graduate courses. The Centre is making its own contribution in this direction.

(*v*) **Training and consultation for other organisations and countries** : There is an infinite market for continuing education and the Centre, because of its innovative experience, gives its help and advice to other organisations and universities in Australia and elsewhere.

(*vi*) **Self-directed study and library visits programme** : Here the Centre arranges for people to come and stay at ANU for self-study for short periods.

The following extracts from the 1972 report of the Centre may be of some interest :

(*i*) The programme of refresher and diversification courses is unlikely to increase significantly so long as this work is defined as additional and external to the main teaching task of university lecturers and also until the idea of significant periods of study level becomes more widely accepted throughout society.

(*ii*) The Centre's special competency may be in the arranging of such conferences, seminars or encounters and the study of the purposes and processes of such experiences. The small carefully-designed conferences, often by invitation, are well fitted to examine critical issues in society and to facilitate change where this is desired by the participants who bear particular responsibility for the situation. They involve substantial preparation work to identify all aspects of a problem and at the same time involve participation in advanced agenda-building for the conference. Information is provided through pre-circulated papers, rather than through lectures and most of the work is done by search syndicates, moderated by the Centre staff.

(*iii*) The Centre has developed expertise and reputation in the area of search conferences. Much of its research effort goes into the evaluation and follow-up of such conferences.

(*iv*) Our objective is to develop the educational potential of organisations, including educational, public and professional. Adaptation of individuals or organisations to rapid change implies learning how to learn (attention to educational processes rather than merely to content), and adopting work settings to foster this. We seek to call attention to the need to restructure jobs and organisations so that members and employers can continue to learn through the work. This is allied more closely with IVAN ILLICH's 'philosophy of deschooling society' rather than with the massive credit-bearing extension programmes of many American Universities.

(*v*) The Centre aims to provide a laboratory for the examination of learning environments designed round small largely autonomous groups. The interest is in transferring of learning into the organisational work setting from which participants come.

(*vi*) The small group-learning-training courses examine, through theoretical and practical sessions, the educational potential of a small group as a teaching learning situation and the conceptual basis and assumptions underlying such work.

(*vii*) The Centre is increasingly convinced that it is an infinitely expanding market situation. Far from wishing to draw to its control more and more aspects of continuing education, it considered it essential to help others to do so. The word "consultant" gives an idea of arrogance. The words 'facilitator' and 'animator' do not describe adequately what we wish to do. There is a cooperative relationship in which both parties can contribute and learn.

8. Australian Academy of Sciences

The Australian Academy of Sciences was given the Royal Charter in 1954 and has 163 fellows and 4 corresponding members at present. It can elect 6 fellows in 10 years for conspicuous service to the cause of science or whose election shall be of significant benefit to the Academy and advancement of science. The corresponding members cannot be more than 1/10th of the number of fellows at any time. The Academy is housed in an architecturally nice building with a lake on one side, with a water canal around the building, with a nice auditorium, a fellow's room and a library for the history of science in Australia. The Academy does not publish journals of its own but actively cooperates with the CSIRO in the Board of Standards whose duty is to see that high standards are maintained in all journals published by the CSIRO. It has published 17 reports on technical and educational matters, 8 science and industry reports and has also published proceedings of a large number of symposia conducted by it.

9. **Australian National Library**

It has a beautiful marble-slab building with the lake on one side and fountains and extensive lawns on the other and having a commanding view of the mountains at a distance. It currently houses a total collection of about 10 lakh volumes, 16,000 bound volumes of newspapers, 4,500,000 ft. of microfilms, documents and newspapers, 4,500 historical prints, drawings and photographs, 1,000 shelf feet of manuscripts, 11,500,000 ft. of moving picture films, 75,000 movie stills, 1,200,000 maps, 400,000 aerial photographs and a growing collection of sound recordings.

The library has 50,000 pages of works of Mahatma Gandhi, 220 original Indian paintings, a large number of Indian newspapers (some of which reach there by air), collection of debates of Indian Legislative Council and Indian Parliament from 1867 onwards.

The readers do not have direct access to all books. A reader gives a slip at the counter; the slip is put in a cylindrical box which is transported mechanically to the floor where the book is located. The attendant picks up the slip, traces out the book and puts it on a belt which brings it down to the counter. This operation may take 10-15 minutes. When the book arrives at the counter, its call number is flashed on a screen so that the waiting reader can go to the counter and collect the book,

The Oriental section of the library has 100,000 books in Chinese, Japanese, Thai and Korean. This is one of the largest collections of such books at one place outside these countries. There are books on arts and newspapers in all these languages. There is a Chinese typewriter which has 3 plates with 400 symbols. Its rare book section contains books about the Benaras uprising and the Impeachment of Warren Hastings printed in India on 1786 and 1789 respectively. There are huge sliding trays for keeping maps and huge sliding panels for keeping paintings. There is a chemical laboratory where old paintings are resurrected and made fit for preservation. There is a section preparing microfilms, microfiche and ultra fiche and there is a number of machines for reading from them.

10. ANU Education Research Unit

The Education Research Unit of the Research School of Social Sciences was established in 1968 and its broad focus of research is Education and Society. About equal emphasis is given on problems of higher and secondary education. The main projects are professional socialisation, human curiosity and intrinsic motivation of students, allocation of resources and cost-benefit analysis of higher education, pressure groups and educational policy. Commonwealth involvement in education, training and adaptation of overseas students, legal aspects of education and regional colleges of advanced education and their environment.

Just as we have small single-faculty affiliated colleges in India, in Australia also there are a number of small single-discipline colleges of advanced education which are not academically or economically viable but which are rooted in the affection of the community they serve. The research unit is looking into their problems through data collection and visits on the lines of the Depth Study conducted by the Meerut University a few years back. Morale of teachers and job-satisfaction in smaller institutions are also being studied. Another subject of study is: Why do students choose a certain professional career and how does their training fit them for the professional career ? The influence of students, teachers, politicians, etc., on educational policy is also being studied. The Centre-

States relationships in financing school and university education and their important role in educational policy are being scrutinised. About 5% of students in higher education are from overseas. Some of them start their education at the school stage here. Their adaptation to Australian condition and their desire to stay on after completing their education are being investigated. The unit includes an Indian research scholar and active members of the Commonwealth Advisory Committee on Research and Development in Education and of the recently formed Higher Education and Research Development Society of Australia (HERDSA)

11. Australian Universities Commission

The AUC was given the responsibility to ensure a 'balanced' development of all Australian universities. It makes recommendations every 3 years for grants to be given to the universities. In the first year it gets submission from the universities, in the second year it visits the universities, and holds discussion with State Governments and in the third year it makes its recommendation and the Commonwealth Government gives its final approval. All the building plans have to be approved by the AUC and its Vice-Chairman is himself a civil engineer. The AUC differs from the Indian UGC in the following respects :

(i) It does not itself distribute money. It recommends to the Commonwealth government which gives money to state Governments to be passed on to the universities.

(ii) It holds direct discussions with the State Governments and gets their approval in advance for whatever it recommends. On academic problems it seeks the advice of the Australian Vice-Chancellors, Committee and usually does not appoint committees of its own.

(iii) It has no direct responsibility for any university, unlike the UGC which is responsible for the Central universities.

(iv) It is concerned with medical, agricultural and technical education also.

16

EDUCATION AND RESEARCH ACTIVITIES IN MELBOURNE

1. **The University of Melbourne**

The university started in 1855 with 3 professors and 16 students with the motto : "I shall grow in the estimation of further generations." Today the university does have an international reputation. It has more than 15,000 students. It covers an area of only 47 acres in the heart of the main city. Its different buildings show the architectural development of Australia during the last 120 years. Its annual recurring income from government grants and students fees exceeds Rs. 22 crores. The main hall has a 30 ft. high mural respresenting humanity struggling out of the primitive ignorance towards knowledge symbolised by the light of the Sun. Its union building which will be 13 storeys high will have canteen, club facilities, library, art gallery, music room, theatres and a big union theatre. The gymnasium with an indoor swimming pool was donated by one man and so was the library building which has now more than 5 lakh books.

2. **Yoga movement in Australia**

In most of the Australian universities, the Indian influence was felt through either the small number of Indian faculty members or the very large posters on Yoga. The three movements which appear to be popular are :

(a) Hare Krishna movement;

(b) The transcendental meditation of Mahesh Yogi ; and

(c) The Divine Light Mission of Balyogeshwar.

There was some opposition in the press to Hare Krishna movement asking why the government could not ban begging in the streets. There were many classes for explaining meditation and the philosophy of Balyogeshwar.

3. Centre for study of Higher Education

This Centre was established in 1968 after amalgamating the audiovisual section, the education research office and the university teaching office established earlier. The Centre carries on research in examinations, educational techniques, computer teaching and evaluation techniques and works in close collaboration with teaching and academic departments to improve teaching and learning situations. It offers an in-service course for academic staff which consists of an intensive course for one week for three hours per day before the beginning of the first term and subsequent 1½ hours' sessions on 5 days in each of the three terms. In the intensive seasons, the topics discussed include learning by students, testing, large group teaching, educational technology, small group learning, etc., while the discussions in the rest of the year are concerned with discussions on topics like motivation to learn, student discipline, workload, continuous assessment, creativity, intelligence and academic performance, programmed instruction, setting examinations, marking examinations, supervision of research, university administration, etc.

The Centre has published a report on the feasibility of Australian Open University and has undertaken projects on student workloads and study habits and on laboratories in professional courses. It has published a book "An assessment of university teaching" in collaboration with the Society for Research in Higher Education, which is a society which holds annual conferences, organises study groups, issues abstracts of research, publishes reports and monographs, etc. It has published principles and technology of undergraduate examinations giving advice about setting of papers and evaluation. It has carried out a survey of the social background of students joining university and on graduation rates of the students. It has installed a student feedback system in a lecture theatre. Here on each seat there are 5 buttons. When a teacher asks a multiple-type objective question during the course of the lesson, each student presses the button and the lecturer knows immediately how many have understood and he can adjust his teaching accordingly. Research work on microteaching with audiovisual tapes is also being done. The Centre also helps teachers who are interested in self-assessment in preparing questionnaires to be filled by students and then advising the teachers about possible improvements in their teaching.

4. **Monash University Centre for Higher Education**

Its activities are : (i) *technical research and development in teaching techniques,* *e.g.*, in reading efficiency of the students, (ii) *educational surveys* on problems posed by the university or departments or even student groups, *e.g.*, load imposed by courses on students, social composition of incoming student population, use of TV in the university, (iii) *educational practices advisory service* which includes organisation of forums, seminars, workshops, publication of 'notes on higher education' and advice to teachers to improve their teaching through experience in microteaching. The Centre also conducts a diploma in education specifically for the tertiary teachers. The course based on part-time study provides for two semesters dealing with theoretical aspects of tertiary education as well as additional two semesters providing the knowledge and practice in various teaching methods. The centre also conducts orientation courses for fresh teachers. It has conducted small-group discussion on tutorials, lecturing, examination, etc.

5. **Victoria Institute of Colleges (V.I.C.)**

This Institute is like an affiliating university with 15 technical, arts and crafts and para-medical colleges which conduct their own examinations under the supervision of the Institute. The courses of study are determined by the Institute. The teachers of the colleges are not represented on the Boards of Studies or Committees of the Institute unless they are experts in their own right. The budget for the 15 colleges is about Rs. 50 crores per year. The Vice-President of the Institute has powers similar to those of the Vice-Chancellor of an affiliating university in India.

6. **Council of Adult Education (CAE)** :

The CAE renders the following services to the community of Melbourne :

(i) *The discussion groups service* helps people to organise informal discussion groups in their own homes. Boxes consisting of books or records or boxes with a mixture of books, music records, etc., are sent to one of the members of the group who acts as a secretary and whose duty is to receive, distribute and return the materials to the Council and handle correspondence on behalf of the group. 6 is the minimum number for a group and 15 is the maximum. Fee for a member is $ 4 a year and postage on boxes is paid by the Council. In return, each member receives on loan in a year about 11 books and notes on them for reading and discussion. Some of the groups continue to work for years together.

(ii) *The Schools and conference service* section organises seminars, conferences, one-day and week-end classes, both residential and non-residential. An annual two-week summer school in January involves several hundred persons in creative classes and lecture discussions.

(iii) *Drama tutorial service* gives advice on speech, movement, testing, lighting, scene, etc., both for professional and amateur groups. It also provides slides, tape-recording on make-up and design, etc., and on some standard plays.

(iv) *The library service* provides access to a well-stocked library of books, records, etc., free to students and at nominal cost to others.

(v) *Regular course of one night a week* or $1\frac{1}{2}$ hours to 3 hours as well as more extensive course for part-time students. The fee charged is roughly Rs. 6/- for one night which meets 50% of the cost and the rest is met by the Government. Courses are also offered for high school adult students. Some of the new courses offered in 1973 by the Council were : Australian

Social History, Australian Politics, Aborigines, Asian Politics, Japan, Bangla Desh, Ireland 1673-1800, Advanced Environmental Ecology, Pornography, Philosophy, Moral Ideals and Political Necessity, Political Concepts and Conflicts, Philosophy of Mathematics, Kant's Moral Philosophy, Philosophy of Religion, the Mystical Language and Philosophy, Christian Theology, Bhagwat Gita, Religion and Society in China and India, Mathematical Dragon-Hunting, Man and his Environment, Contemporary French Literature, Modern Art, Audio-Visual Media, Italian, Japanese, Spanish, Afrikan, Physiology, Mathematics for Parents, Indian Cooking, Chinese Cooking, Javanese Dancing, Painting of dolls and puppets, Silk Screen Printing. Other interesting courses are: Destiny of Man, Comparative Religion, Operations Research, Data Processing, Computer Programming, Birds Study, Nutrition, Theatres, Learning to Study, Public Speaking, Chinese, French, German, Greek, Hebrew, Hindi, Indonesian, Italian, Swedish, Understanding Children Behaviour, Making Your Own Furniture, Gardening, Wine Appreciation, Running a small Business. The Efficient Secretary, Piano, Drawing, Painting, Pottery, Geology, Rug Weaving, Photography, Fencing, Wood work, Keeping Fit.

7. **Department of Indian Studies of Melbourne University**

This Department teaches about 150 students in the first year and about Rs. 50 crores will be spent on its development programmes during the next 10 years. Its full-time and part-time students number about 8,000. Its emphasis is on applied science and technology. The research, its faculty members do, is also of immediate relevance. It has an efficient computer system and is going to get a bigger computer system in the near future worth about Rs. 1 crore.

8. **La Trobe University**

This is the newest university in Melbourne and was started about 1966. Its lecture hall system is interesting in the sense that there are six lecture halls and there is a central projection room from where films and slides can be projected on the screen in the lecture halls. The projector operator uses a mirror so that the picture on the transparent screen appears reversed to himself, but is all right for the viewers in the lecture theatre.

Films and slides can be shown simultaneously in all the six lecture theatres. There is a control panel for the lecture from where the lecturer can speak to the projection operator and can switch on and off the lights, can use the overhead projector and can operate the huge sliding black-boards. The library at La Trobe University has 175,000 books at present. Out of 5,000 students at the university, about 1,000 live on the campus in a number of colleges. Since the university is far away from the city, the teachers and other students go away and except for the library, the university presents a dead appearance on Saturdays and Sundays. The organisation and the government of La Trobe University is typical of what is evolving in many universities. (See page 101).

9. School of Education of La Trobe University

The school has at present 42 faculty members and plans to have 86 in the near future. At present it has the following 5 centres :

(i) **Centre for Comparative and International Studies in Education**

This Centre aims to make careful examination and evaluation of educational trends in Europe, USA, Asian and Pacific countries. One basic objective of the Centre is to develop a series of comparative and international studies of education systems of neighbouring countries and to contribute to methodological development of the education discipline. The Centre is multidisciplinary as well as cross-cultural in its outlook.

(ii) **Centre for the Study of Educational Communication and Media**

Communication research has become in recent years one of the front line areas in the study of human behaviour. Communication of knowledge from one person to another is the basis of teaching. Mass media are major sources of information and attitude change outside schools. Various forms of educational technology are being used increasingly in schools themselves. The Centre hopes to carry out systematic research in learning, but such questions as the efficiency of the communication process in teaching, the effect of mass media on knowledge and attitude and habits, comparison of mass media influence with the influence of the school, understanding media and educational technology, ways of assisting teachers to use educational technology, efficiently and evaluation of their effects. Research projects are already in progress on the role of microteaching, on improvement of teaching preformance at mass media, portrayal of violence and aggression, teachers' attitude to TV, etc.

(iii) **Centre for the Study of Innovations in Education**

This Centre intends to develop two main lines of activity. The first will involve the sponsorship, development and analysis of substantial innovations by or through the Centre while the second line of investigation will be involved with the process of innovation itself and might invoke study of successful and unsuccessful innovations of the past or present and the study of success of an innovation as it depends on the mode of introducing the innovation or on the source from which this arises.

(iv) **Centre for the Study of Teaching**

The orientation of this Centre will be towards the conceptualisation of a global theory of the teaching-learning process embracing associated problems such as the nature of the teachers' role and effectiveness, communication in the human groups, analysis of teaching on the basis of preparation of teachers, effectiveness of teaching procedures, study of creative processes in teaching and the means of facilitating both creative learning environment and creative behaviour.

(v) **Centre for the Study of Urban Education**

The Centre is concerned with the study of inequality and disadvantage in education within the urban setting and the pattern of form of education best suited to urban life. The Centre intends to discover the links between the environmental and educational problems and the urban process which lies behind them.

Organisation of La Trobe University

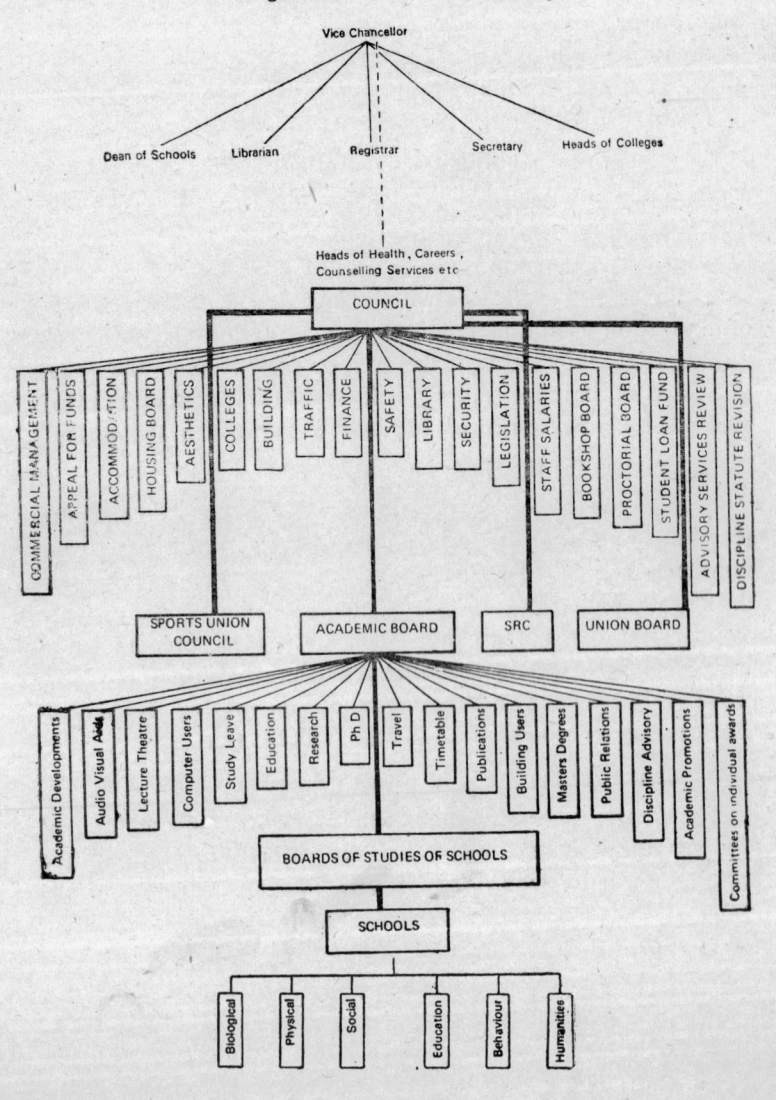

17

EDUCATION AND RESEARCH ACTIVITIES IN SYDNEY, NEWCASTLE, TOWNSVILLE AND BRISBANE

1. **The University of Sydney**

This is the oldest university in Australia having been established in 1852 and thus is older than the oldest university established in modern times in 1857 in India. Its budget is Rs. 42 crores per year. Its main building completed in 1859 is a good example of Gothic revival architecture. It has both modern and old buildings side by side, but efforts have been made to see that the modern buildings are grafted nicely into the old building so that there is a pleasant effect. Its mathematics department building is named after late Prof. Carlsaw, the author of 'Fourier Series and Integrals' who taught here in the beginning of the century and the centenary of whose birth was celebrated appropriately by the department last year. The department has interests in pure mathematics, applied mathematics and statistics.

2. **Department of Adult Education, University of Sydney**

The department, started in 1913, has a budget of Rs. 40 lakhs of which the government gives Rs. 11.5 lakhs, Rs. 7.9 lakhs comes from fees and about Rs. 21 lakhs comes from university funds. During 1972 its activities were : (i) 153 classes in Sydney with 4,880 enrolments, (ii) 62 classes in other parts of New South Wales with 1,280 enrolments, (iii) 42 weekly programmes of TV lessons with estimated 60,000 viewers, (iv) 295 discussion groups with 490 courses, 2,990 students and 4,820 enrolments, (v) publication of "Current Affairs Bulletin" with 35,000 subscribers, (vi) 5 schools and conferences for general public with 630 students, (vii) aboriginal adult education and community advancement programmes, (viii) Master of Education Seminar on Adult Education, (ix) Special lectures.

In the tutorial classes philosophy, logic and religion accounted for 15.5% enrolment, science for 10.6%, social sciences for 15.5%, arts and architecture for 5.4%, history and international affairs for 27.7%, literature and drama for 7.8%, foreign languages for 8.1%, while in the discussion groups 37% were in literature, 6% were in arts and architecture, 5% were in music, 9% were in psychology and education, 9% were in science, 15% were in social sciences, 5% were in history and 12% were in philosophy and religion. The widely different percentages in the two groups of learners lead to interesting conclusions.

3. **University of New South Wales**

Though it was established only in 1949, it is the largest university with an enrolment of more than 19,000 students. The university plans to have ultimately 20,000 students of whom 5,000 will be post-graduate. The university established in 1959, Unistarch Ltd., a company wholly owned and controlled by the University to assist Australian industry in the solution of research and development problems. The university has faculties of applied science, architecture, arts, biological sciences, commerce, engineering, law, medicine and military studies. It has also a board of vocational studies and another board of studies in general education and a tertiary education and research centre. The university has courses in wool technology, ceramics, engineering, polymers, optometry, textile technology and fuel technology at the undergraduate level and business administration, nuclear engineering, traffic engineering and highway engineering at the post-graduate level.

The University has an open day on the first September when each department put up programmes for the students and the members of the public. These include demonstrations on minicomputers, remote time-sharing control, hovercrafts, mixed media applications, night driving, simulation, architectural models, herbarium display, computer art, films on various academic topics and university activities, language laboratory, information retrieval, desk calculators, educational technology and even kite flying for children.

4. **University of New Castle**

This university with about 4,000 students only has spent about 20 million dollars on its buildings so far. A new medical school has been sanctioned and this is taken to mean that the university has come of age. Its Great Hall was constructed at a cost of a million dollars. The university has a nice campus with tall trees all around. Some of the work done in the university on mathematical models, mathematical psychology, physical oceanography and combinatorial mathematics has won international recognition. Some work on mathematical psychology with the application of systems theory, differential manifolds and Lie groups to visual perception is also interesting.

5. **James Cook University of North Queensland**

Townsville is a city with a population of about 7,5000 and is one of Australia's fastest growing cities and at present is Australia's largest tropical city with an average temperature of 69° F—80°F. James Cook University of Northern Queensland became Australia's 15th university, and the only tropical university there, on April 20, 1970, though it had operated as a college much earlier. It has 1,500 students and about 200 faculty members. Its computer centre has a PDP-10 system with 24 terminals—4 of these with a screen each. One of these terminals works in the library and in its memory, it has the complete catalogue of more than 100,000 books. As soon as a book is issued or returned, information goes to the computer memory. If one wants to know to whom a book is issued or how many and which books are issued to any one, one can get the information in less than 10 seconds. It has microfilms of a large number of newspapers. One Godrej-type almirah can contain about 2 complete newspapers for about 50 years on microfilm.

The Education Department has interesting programmes of B.Ed. (Hons.) and M.Ed. (Hons.). M.Ed. can be done both by course work and by theses.

The Supervision of teacher-pupils is done by master teachers of cooperative schools. The master teachers get remuneration and the principals of the schools concerned nominate them. This system has produced a great deal of cooperation between practising schools and the university department. This also relieves the university teachers from other work and produces a uniform teaching schedule throughout the year. There were videotapes arrangements in all the practising schools so that the teaching of each teacher-pupil could be videotaped and his teaching could later be discussed by the university faculty. The teaching of the university faculty was also sometimes videotaped and discussed by the students and the faculty. This equipment was also used for a project on the education of the special learning disability children in the clinic of the department. The computer centre has a large system for the small enrolment of students, but it is expecting to increase its capacity to six times during the next six years and to replace the present computer altogether after 10 years.

There is a comparative education society which discusses educational systems of various countries.

6. University of Queensland

This has a number of Indian professors in some departments and there was a great deal of interest in application of mathematics and mathematics education in the mathematics department.

18

COMPARATIVE STUDY OF AUSTRALIAN AND INDIAN SYSTEMS OF HIGHER EDUCATION

1. **Resources for Higher Education in Australia**

There are 15 universities in Australia at present and three more are going to be started during the next three years. The number of students in a university varies from 1,500 to 18,000 though most of the universities have between 5,000 to 10,000 students. The annual budget of a university varies from Rs. 5 crores to Rs. 30 crores and most of the universities have their budgets between Rs. 10-20 crores. The number of books in the university libraries varies from 1 lakh to about 10 lakhs. The expenditure per student is roughly about Rs. 20,000 per year and is almost uniform all over the country except at the Institute of Advanced Studies in Australian National University which is a purely research organisation, where the expenditure per research student may come to about Rs. 75,000 per year.

As against this, the expenditure per student in India comes to about Rs. 600 per student. The number of students in a university may be as high as 2-3 lakhs. The number of books and journals in the libraries is much smaller. We have, however IIT's, medical colleges and agricultural universities and some central universities where the expenditure per student is relatively high and may be as high as Rs. 5,000 to Rs. 15,000 p.a.; yet the average expenditure is not at all comparable with the average expenditure in Australia.

2. Respect for Higher Education in Australia

There is fundamental belief in Australian society that quality higher education is the indispensable means for developing human resources which will in turn enable the country to exploit the natural resources of the country. Investment in higher education is considered to be the most profitable investment for the country. Research in universities is regarded as vital for the progress of the nation. University professors are very often consulted by the government on all important economic, social and scientific problems, before it takes policy decisions and the government values the advice given. The large funds that are available to the universities are mostly due to this philosophy about higher education which influences both the government and the public.

On the other hand in India, universities do not get that respect. Political parties are prepared to exploit university students and teachers for their own ends and nobody worries seriously if universities are closed for months together. There is more emphasis on the advice of the bureaucrats than on the advice of the university professors, though there are some exceptions. Many students come to the university not because they are interested in higher education but because they have nothing else to do. In the absence of full employment for graduates, there is lack of motivation on the part of the students and lack of commitment on the part of the teachers. Sometimes the atmosphere appears quite unrealistic and at places higher education looks more as a ritual than as a fundamental necessity for national prosperity.

As a contrast, the high respect in which universities are held in Australia and the great expectations from them are clear from the following extracts from a recent speech by Mr. Whitlam, the former Prime Minister of Australia.

(i) All governments have accorded to the universities an autonomy, a status and a financial security in keeping with their importance as defenders of certain primary intellectual and civilised values.

(ii) The quality which distinguishes most a free society from the totalitarian is the existence of free universities. Academic freedom is the first requirement, the essential property of a free society.

(iii) Until a generation ago, the classic stance of the university, its real and popular image was that of an institution isolated, remote and apart from the currents and pressures of the world. In its separation lay its strength. It was a guarantee of its independence. It enabled universities to survive as sanctuaries of scholarship and intellectual dissent in spite of political vicissitudes and at times totalitarian systems that would have crushed them.

(iv) The universities today exist in a more propitious social and political climate. They can no longer be the sequestered retreats of intellectual or cultivated elites.

(v) Where once the strength of the university lay in isolation, it lies now in participation, in a process of organic involvement with the needs and aspirations of society.

(vi) While universities are almost totally dependent on public funds, at the same time, governments depend more and more on universities for advice and research. The universities must participate more readily in the solution of current problems and seek a more relevant and contemporary role as organs of public service.

(vii) Academics are uniquely equipped by training and temperament to evaluate evidence to assess priorities, initiate speculative and creative lines of research on ways that can help governments to transform broad policy concepts into detailed working models for legislative action.

(viii) Modern government would be impossible without a corpus of expert advice from outside—advice formulated with none of the restraints, scruples or professional discipline, imposed on even the best trained and most dedicated civil service.

(*ix*) It is not sufficient that universities create an informed and literate population or that individuals should perform specific tasks as government advisers. To fulfil their true role as "Independent centres far-ranging thought", they must assume the duties of social critics.

(*x*) I want academics to stimulate public awareness and understanding of social issues. It is not enough that they should be centres of isolated protest or demonstration. We need universities working peacefully in society and in harmony with elected governments. Academics should be "unacknowledged legislators of mankind".

(*xi*) Tertiary education in whatever form must be as accessible and as integral a part of the range of public instruction as education of any other kind. Our purpose should be not only to augment the output of trained graduates to meet the country's needs and not merely to promote quality. The purpose is to involve the universities and the communities they serve, more closely in each other's welfare, to draw the universities more deliberately into a deliberate and participative commitment to the public good.

(*xii*) We live in a world in which the frontiers of knowledge are expanding. In the Western world, the critical indicators, *viz.*, scientific education, investment, publications, the number of men trained, percentage of gross national product committed to research and development are doubling every 7-10 years. No previous period in history offers any parallel to the current exponential growth in the rate, multiplication and effect of scientific and technological advance.

(*xiii*) One of our urgent concerns must be whether our institutions and systems of education are equipped to handle this growth without the catastrophic collapse in the traditional method of teaching and research.

(*xiv*) With this growth in knowledge, there is a matching growth in bafflement and frustration. The problems faced not just by us, but by humanity, are of a new order and scale : growing urbanisation, mounting population pressures, rapidly diminishing resources, widespread hunger and pollution, a rampant technology heedless of our natural environment and delicate ecological balance, the vast destructive potential of our modern armaments, the challenge to human values and human freedom by a growing multi-national industrial technocracy. In such situations, human instinct may turn to increasing totalitarian solutions to even more oppressive form of tyranny and regimentation.

(xv) Against these threats to civilisation, the universities will be our last, perhaps our only defence. The values they embody, namely, those of knowledge and truth and freedom must prevail, if man has to avert disaster. It remains a matter of conjecture whether free universities as we know them will survive in the 21st century. If they do, they will not be as cloistered retreats of a privileged few. They will be man's chief ally in the struggle to preserve our freedom and our species from destruction.

The above statements reflect the official and national policy statements of the attitude of the Australian government to universities and account for the vast resources that have been made available for the growth and development of universities in Australia and for the realisation on the part of the academic community that they must play an increasingly vital role in the development of their nation. When this attitude is compared with the attitude in India, where university education is given low priority, where universities' advice is seldom sought on national problems, and where universities are regarded as places for disgruntled youth and faculty, we can easily see the reason for the lack of resources for the Indian universities. Our great leader Pandit Nehru had, however, a similar vision of a university when he declared : "The university stands for humanism, for tolerance, for reason, for progress, for the adventure of ideas and for the search of truth. It stands for the onward march of the human race towards even higher objectives. If the universities discharge their duties adequately, then it is well with the nation and the people."

In the beginning, our universities received resources for development, but later on these resources were used for developing big national laboratories and research organisations which weakened the universities both in manpower and in resources. Today the amounts allotted to universities for research are so pitifully small, even in comparison to the total national resources for research and development, that it is not surprising that Indian universities have been unable to play their role of the type envisaged by Mr. Whitlam and Pandit Nehru. Universities must be given the respect and must deserve the respect, for the progress of the nation.

3. Research in higher education

We have given in earlier chapters the work done by the education research units in Australian universities. We have similar problems in our country and educational research in these areas is extremely important. Universities should be encouraged to start higher education research units with the twin objectives of doing research in problems of higher education and of improving the teaching-learning situations in classrooms by using modern pedagogic and technological tools.

4. Part-time vocational training for in-service technicians

Every skilled worker in Australia has to be an apprentice for certain number of years and during this period he receives a training normally for one day a week at government expense and only after the successful completion, he gets a licence to independently practise. This leads to a great deal of efficiency on the part of the skilled workers. In our case persons do become apprentices and learn something from the master skilled workers, but no theoretical or professional training is given so that failures occur at critical points. It is necessary that there should be an element of compulsion in requiring that persons should acquire technical qualifications and at the same time training facilities specially for in-service and part-time persons be provided on a large scale. Our weakest links in the industrial chain today are the middle-level technicians and the weakness arises because of the lack of facilities and motivation for in-service training.

5. Continuing and Adult Education in Australian Universities

Australian universities and state departments for continuing education cater on a large scale to the desire of the community for continuing education. Many universities arrange hundreds of courses of 10-50 lectures each on various topics of interest to the adult citizens. These include courses on foreign languages, cooking, dress-making, secretarial practices, international politics, flora and fauna of Australia, pollution, sociology, religion and civilization. In addition to these evening lectures, universities provide for discussion groups in remote areas where books and notes are sent every month to interested groups of 10-15 people who are interested in continuing their education. About half the cost of the courses is met by the participants and half is met by the State.

In India only 3-4 universities have made some efforts in continuing education. For the success of this effort, we need to create an interest in life-long education and even in paying for it and we need a massive effort on the part of the universities which should feel that their responsibility for higher education extends to not only people in the age group 17-23, but they are responsible for the education of everybody in the age group 17-70 or even possibly beyond.

We have the Indian Council of Adult Education and the Indian Universities Association for Continuing Education, but obviously efforts on a much greater scale are necessary. There should be State Councils of Adult Education in every state and every university should have a department of continuing education and efforts should be made on the same scale as in Australia.

6. Colleges of Advanced Education in Australia and Community Autonomous Colleges for India

Australia does not have affiliated colleges like ours. On the other hand, it has about 100 autonomous colleges which determine their own admission policies and conduct their own examinations. They are not autonomous as far as curriculum making is concerned, but the curricula are not decided by some central authority. The teachers of each college propose curricula in the light of the needs of the community in which the college is situated, but the curricula have to be approved by the representatives of the community. There are representatives of business, industry, various professions and others who decide whether the curricula are according to the needs of the society. All these colleges give what is called need-based education.

The phrase "job-oriented" education is not used in Australia since a job is available for every one. However, education is given to meet the needs of skilled workers in Australian industry. These colleges also offer part-time courses in the evening for improving the efficiency of workers in all walks of life and quite a large percentage of the working population attends these colleges for part time courses for at least two hours a week. These courses are tailor-made to suit the needs of these groups. In fact, if an industry or a business group wants a specific type of training for its workers, the colleges are always ready to make the arrangements for the same. About 40% of the teachers in these colleges are those who have had at least 5 years' experience in business, commerce, banking, insurance, government or industry. These colleges do not undertake academic research but are otherwise completely integrated with the life of the community. Some of these colleges are quite big and have budgets of Rs. 8-10 crores per year and may have three to five thousand full-time students and five to seven thousand part-time students.

In India 85% of the students study in affiliated colleges whose admission policies, examinations and syllabi are governed by central bodies. Few teachers of these colleges have any experience outside the college or the university and as such are not in a position to implement the policy of job-oriented courses about which there is so much talk. There are no members of the community associated with syllabi making. Though there are some members of the community associated with Executive Councils, and University Courts, their representation in academic bodies is insignificant. While the members of the community feel that the present courses are too academic, they cannot change these courses. The academic community, while it may pay lip sympathy to vocational courses or need-based courses, is not in a position to implement such a programme. We should convert at least 100 of our colleges every year into autonomous colleges with the directive that they will give job-oriented, need-based courses and for this purpose persons from industry, business, commerce, agriculture, etc., should be actively associated with the framing of the curricula for these colleges. All new colleges should be autonomous and with need-based syllabi. In the first instance, universities may start autonomous institutions of this type, but great efforts will have to be made to see that the syllabi do not become carbon copies of the present syllabi for the sake of academic respectability or due to the academic inertia of the teachers who may not be ready to learn and teach need-based courses. Just as the government is planning for a model school in every district, it should have at least a model college of a new type in every division in the country in the next Five Year Plan. The courses given in Australian colleges of Advanced and technical education given earlier in the essay are indicative of need-based courses and we can easily draw up courses to meet our requirements.

7. Applied Bias in Research

Though there is a great deal of fundamental research in Australia and quite a number of Australians have won Nobel Prizes, yet most of the research in Australian Universities is on significant national problems. Even in mathematics departments 40-50% of the theses are written on problems of physical, oceanography, thermal pollution, operations research, computer mathematics, biomathematics, mathematics of mines and metallurgy, town-planning, river flows and so on. The inspiration for research comes mostly from the life of the community and not so much from the research problems being tackled in USA or USSR. There is a great pressure for publication, but there is a greater pressure for useful publications.

In India, on the other hand, research is more often motivated by the desire to publish or to improve upon the research originating in Western countries than by the needs of our own society. It is more difficult and requires greater originality to work on meaningful problems arising out of our own local and national needs than to work on extensions of research done in other countries; but unfortunately though we are politically independent, we have not really become independent in our research. We require greater originality and courage in our research work.

Our research workers should cease worrying about international recognition and should engage themselves in solving thousands of problems round them which will win them national affection and regard.

8. Student unrest and student participation

About three years ago there were agitations in most of the universities in Australia on two main issues—one was the Vietnamwar and the other was student participation. The first issue isnow dead and the second was decided by giving students participation in all university bodies, including the Executive Councial faculties and the academic Council. Usually the students have 5-10% of the seats in these bodies. Their contribution has been quite healthy. At present there are no signs of student unrest.

The other causes which cause student unrest in India are almost absent there. Thus every university there has a union building, which may be 10-11 storeys high, containing canteen, indoor sports facilities, theatres, bookshops, banks, etc., and Australian students cannot complain of lack of physical amenities. The papers are always set by the teachers who teach them and therefore there is no question of papers being out of course. The answer books are returned to the students and so there is no question of partiality in evaluation. Every student is almost sure of employment and therefore there is full motivation for study. Teachers get good salaries and promotions are usually decided by their colleagues on merit without outside interference. The criteria for promotion are usually objective in terms of publications and reputation as a teacher. Political parties have enough respect for the universities and they do not usually exploit the universities. The gross inequalities in income which are so evident in India are not there in Australia. Leaving aside 20% people who may be very rich or very poor, 80% of the people have their ratio of income as 1:4. There is affluence and almost every family has two cars. There is human dignity for every one and manual work is respected. The tremendous inequalities in income which make our students rebel are not there. The students are too excited about modern developments in knowledge to deviate towards agitations There is some generation gap but the older generation is trying to accommodate itself to the aspirations of the younger generation. Corruption, nepotism and favouritism which make our youngmen angry and frustrated are very insignificant.

9. **Emphasis on computer**

In all the universities and technical colleges in Australia the emphasis is on doing all operations and giving all possible training with the latest computers. Australia is also importing computers but because of shortage of manpower it believes in doing everything possible with the aid of computers. In our country, for large scale organisations, we need computers and there should be greater emphasis on computer training and research.

10. **Research in resources and environmental problems**

Research in and optimum utilisation of all resources and of preventing pollution of air, land and water are given the highest priority there. For us also it is very important that our limited resources are used in the best possible manner and we take steps to keep our environment clean.

11. **Strengthening of Association of Indian Universities**

The Australian Vice-Chancellors Committee is very powerful and its opinions on all academic matters are heard with a great deal of respect. Our Association of Indian Universities should also cease to be a Vice-Chancellors' club and should aim to have a decisive influence on higher educacation policy in the country.

12. **Balanced Development of Universities**

Australian Universities Commission has been given the responsibilities of ensuring balanced development of all universities and as such the resources and standards of all Australian universities are more or less comparable. Of course each university may have some departments of a very high standard and the Commission helps the university to develop these departments further, but then the centres of excellence are also evenly spread over all the universities. The only exception is the Institute of Advanced Studies which is regarded as a national organisation.

In India, the UGC has the responsibility of maintaining the central universities and a major portion of its budget is spent on them. From the remaining, it has to help in the development of more than 80 universities. Instead of ensuring the balanced development of Indian universities the UGC has become an instrument of producing inequalities in educational opportunities and in resources available to the universities. The responsibility for maintaining the central universities should not be with the UGC, otherwise it is not possible for it to ensure balanced development. The present situation is also misleading as it makes the nation believe that the central government is assisting all the universities. The resources at the disposal of the various universities should be the same and centres of excellence should be distributed in all the universities. The best policy would be to ask each state to contribute a certain percentage of its budget for higher education and the central government should also contribute a similar percentage. All these funds should be placed at the disposal of the central UGC which should distribute these funds equitably without making any distinction between central and state universities and in such a way as to ensure a balanced development of all universities in India. An alternative method is to make higher education a central subject and ask the states to concentrate all their resources on education up to the higher secondary level only.

13. **Some suggestions for higher education and research in India in the light of the Australian experience**

(*i*) Every teacher in a college or a university should have a separate room for himself on the campus. We may need about one lakh of rooms whose cost may be about Rs. 50 crores though it may be considerably reduced if proper design can be evolved. There should be shelves for keeping books and each teacher should be expected to stay for 8 hours a day in his office, studying and discussing with the students. At present every college has a large staff room where no serious work can be done with the result that teachers are not even inclined to stay in the college after their lectures are over. This reduces the student-teacher contact to a minimum. In Australia every teacher stays in his office from 8.30 a.m. to 5.00 p m. and is available to the students in his office on appointment. For the rest of the time, he studies in his office. Only academic discussions take place in the offices. For non-academic discussions, the teachers go to the common rooms.

(*ii*) Every teacher should have a library of his own and he should be given books at heavily subsidised rates. The income-tax exemption limit should be 10% of the salary in the case of teachers.

(*iii*) There should be a mass production programme of books on a large scale in all languages and cheaper books, both for students and teachers, should be produced. The programme may require an investment of about Rs. 50 crores.

(*iv*) Universities should be encouraged to take continuing and adult education programmes on a large scale. Unemployed young men may be recruited for adult education work and Rs. 50 crores set aside for this purpose. Evening classes on a large scale for all types of workers in factories and offices may be an incentive and may be provided for them to attend these courses to improve their efficiency.

(*v*) No more affiliated colleges should be started. All new colleges should be autonomous community colleges. Even the existing colleges should be converted into autonomous community colleges in a phased manner. An autonomous community college will have the freedom in the policy of admissions and examinations, but its curricula will be framed in consultation with the community it serves. The central government may take up the initiative in setting up a model community college in at least every division in the country on the same lines as it intends to set up model schools. A Brains Trust of people in industry, business, commerce, agriculture, professional and academic life may be set up to draw guide lines for these community colleges.

(*vi*) Students should be given representations in faculties, academic councils and Executive Councils and should be made to feel responsibility to some extent for the educational system. Keeping them out of these bodies only encourages them to be irresponsible critics of the system.

(*vii*) There should be control on admissions according to the facilities available and every college should have a fixed number of seats which may be determined after considering all the facilities it has. About 60% seats may be reserved for merit, 20% for those whose parents did not receive higher education and 20% for other weaker sections of society.

(*viii*) Strong steps should be taken to suppress corruption and nepotism in all walks of life for the sake of the moral health of the students. Those who are concerned about student unrest should set examples of high public conduct and those who have the power should see that others do not get away with practices which do harm to the moral fabric of the young generation.

(*ix*) Research grants to universities should be considerably increased. We are spending about Rs. 200 crores on research and development in various national laboratories and other research organisations, but not even Rs. 10 crores per year are being spent on research in universities. The universities should be given specific research grants for buying costly equipment and a sum of Rs. 50 crores per year sould be given to the universities for research.

(*x*) Correspondence and open university type education should be initiated on a large scale. There may possibly be a separate university in each state for this purpose.

(*xi*) Steps should immediately be taken to ensure the balanced development of the universities. Those universities and colleges which have suffered on account of inadequate resources should be given assistance on a more generous scale than those which have been receiving relatively more generous financial assistance during the past 1-2 decades. Certain minimum standards should be set for every college and university and the index for these may be put as 100. If we do that, we may find some institutions have an index of 30 or 50 and the others have an index of 200 or 250. Those whose index is above 150 may not receive any special assistance; those below 150 should receive special assistance till thus reach the standard of 150 and we should try to ensure that within 5 years, every institution reaches the index of efficiency of 150. This will mean hard and unpopular decisions, but in the interest of education these have to be taken. A similar decision for schools has been taken in Australia and is being enforced against stiff-resistance by vested interests.

(*xii*) Higher education should be made a central subject as soon as possible and national, rather than regional, policies should be pursued in this area. Fortunately education has now come on the concurrent list. This will help the central Government and the UGC, in maintaining and coordinating standards.

14. Concluding remarks

The above schemes may cost about Rs. 500 crores during the next 5 years, but we may consider the alternative of not being able to provide the funds. The alternative will continue to be student unrest, unmotivated students, lack of purpose in higher education and this may also mean that more than Rs. 200 crores on higher education may be wasted per year. Another danger is that the student unrest may explode into undesirable avenues and may endanger the secular, democratic and socialistic character of our country and this damage may be very serious indeed.

Appendix
SOME STATISTICS ABOUT AUSTRALIAN UNIVERSITIES

(1) Enrolments

University	Year of starting	Actual 1972	Estimated 1975	Increase Per cent
NEW SOUTH WALES				
*Sydney	1850	17,112	17,490	2.2
*New South Wales	1858	16,084	17,465	8.6
New England	1954	6,177	7,235	17.1
*New Castle	1964	3,829	4,735	23.7
Macquira	1964	5,781	8,365	44.7
–Wallingong+	1961, 1975	1,510	1,945	28.8
		50,493	57,235	13.4
VICTORIA				
*Melbourne	1853	14,984	15,100	0.8
Monash	1958	11,769	13,160	11.8
*La Trobe	1964	4,039	7,290	80.5
		30,792	35,550	15.5
QUEENSLAND				
*Queensland	1909	17,277	18,440	6.7
*James Cook	1970	1,462	2,085	42.6
Griffith	1975	—	510	—
		18,739	21,035	12.3

Comparative Study of Australian & Indian Systems

SOUTH AUSTRALIA				
*Adelaide	1874	8,404	9,385	11.7
*Flinders	1966	2,489	3,595	44.4
		10,895	12,981	19.2
WESTERN AUSTRALIA				
Western Australia	1911	8,665	10,150	17.1
–Murdoch	1970	—	525	—
		8,665	10,675	23.2
TASMANIA		3,300	4,030	18.9
AUSTRALIAN NATIONAL				
*School	1960	4,768	5,770	21.0
*Institute	1946	336	430	28.0
AUSTRALIA		128,076	147,705	15.3

(ii) **Full-time Staff in Australian Universities :**

Professors	Readers	Sr. Lecturers	Lecturers	Sr. Tutors	Tutors	Total
846	824	2,217	2,356	647	1,352	8,242
10.1%	10.0	26.9	28.6	7.9	16.4	100

(iii) **Percentage increases in number of students in universities :**

1958	1959	1960	1961	1962	1963	1964	1965	1966	1967	1968	1969	1970	1971	1972
13.5	13.6	13.2	8.0	9.8	9.1	10.3	9.4	9.5	3.5	6.1	7.9	6.8	6.1	4.4

(iv) **Tertiary Students in 1971 :**

Universities	Teacher Colleges	CAE	Total
1,22,680	24,250	45,113	1,92,043
%63.99	12.6	23.5	

(v) **Total Government grant :**

1958-60	1960-63	1964-66	1967-69	1970-72	1973-75	
132,385	247,246	377,700	524,827	752,492	101,600	In thousands of dollars
0.53	0.52	0.62	0.67	0.72		as % age of GNP

(vi) **Number of Students per Staff member :**

Agriculture	Arts	Economics	Education	Engineers	Law	Medicine	Science	over-all
7.2	15.3	19.8	14.1	9.9	25.1	8.5	10.5	12.4

(vii) **Growth of Universities :**

In 1959, there were 9 universities with 47,000 students, in 1975 there would be 18 universities with 148,000 students.

*Universities visited   +started as college in 1961   —University is to start functioning from 1975.

19

HIGHER EDUCATION AND RESEARCH IN WEST GERMANY

1. **Purpose.**

I visited the Federal Republic of Germany (F.R.G.) on an invitation from the Cultural Affairs Department of the Federal Foreign Office of the West German Government, as a member of a team of three Vice-Chancellors of Indian Universities (Dr. A. S. Adke, Karnatak University, Dharwar, Dr. Uma Shanker Joshi, Gujarat University, Ahmedabad and myself) and Shri R. K. Chhabra, Secretary, University Grants Commission, New Delhi. The visit was in pursuance of the Cultural Exchange Agreement between the Governments of West Germany and India. Our objects were to study the German system of higher education and research with special reference to recent developments, and to explore the possibilities of mutually beneficial collaboration between West German and Indian universities and scientific organisations. We were in Germany for three weeks, from 18th October 1971 to 6th November 1971 and in this period visited nine universities and five science institutes, and held discussions with a dozen government and non-official organisations concerned with higher education and research.

2. VISIT TO UNIVERSITIES

(i) Technical University, Aachan.

This is a technical university with full-fledged science and humanities departments and with a very good medical faculty. We met here the Rector (Vice-Chancellor), the Chancellor (Registrar) and a number of engineering professors who had visited I.I.T. Madras. It was interesting to know that the Rector of this technical university was a Professor of humanities and the chancellor was getting a higher salary than many secretaries of the federal government. The chancellor was also teaching a regular course of lectures in law. The technical and medical faculties had many joint research projects in biotechnical studies. Every student has to spend six months in industry before joining an engineering course. Every professor has industrial experience and about one-fourth of the lectures are delivered by guest lecturers from industry. The university intends to start soon a diploma (graduate) course in informatics (computer science). The university has 13,000 students and has a large number of buildings spread over a wide area in the centre of the town. I specially visited the computer centre which has equipment worth about 10 crores of rupees, which runs a three-year course for programmes and does thousands of programming jobs per day.

(ii) Free University of Berlin

Since the Von Humboldt University was in East Berlin, this university was established in West Berlin in 1948, after the Second World War, with American help. This has now 18,000 students and 24 departments. We discussed the working of the new university constitution according to which students have about one-third of the seats in the academic senate and the university council. We also visited the Indian Philology Institute where we met German and Indian researchers working on ancient Jain literature.

(iii) Technical University of Berlin

This university has about 10,000 students and has elected a president (instead of Rector) for seven years who was an assistant working for the Ph.D. degree of the same university. The students vote had a definite influence in his election. The university has 21 departments, each of which is run by a council consisting of 7 professors, 4 assistants, 3 students and a non-academic staff member. The Council of the university which elects the president has 42 professors, 42 assistants, 42 students and 20 representatives of the non-academic staff. The final authority is with the Executive Council which has 7 government representatives, 1 professor, 1 assistant, 1 student, 1 non-academic staff member and 3 members elected by the academic senate and the president is not even its member. The council has also elected a vice-president who is a professor and belongs to a different group from that of the president. For appointment of professors, the departmental committee recommends three names, the president approves the list but the final authority of appointment rests with the minister of education of the State.

(iv) **Bonn University**

This is one of the oldest universities with about 18,000 students. We met here an India-born professor of comparative religion, a former Vice-Chancellor who had visited India and a professor who had written a book on Asian art. The University is situated in an old castle of a bishop. We saw a dining room (now used as a lecture hall) where the bishop could be seen eating, by his people, from the balcony, provided the people were properly dressed.

I also visited the Mathematics Institute and had discussions with the Directer about the curriculum and research and the special research grant from the German Research Council of about 25 lakhs of rupees per year which enables the Institute to get guest professors from abroad. I also discussed with Prof. Vogal of the Applied Mathematics Institute the work being done in Operations Research.

(v) **Ruhr University, Bochum**

This is a recently established university in the highly industrialised area of the Ruhr valley, primarily for sons and daughters of the industrial workers. It has 13 buildings of 13 storeys each and in addition has 110 lecture halls and other faculties for students. The cost of construction of the buildings is of the order of Rs. 400 crores and buildings are made of standard prefabricated slabs manufactured at site; the outer structure of each 13 storeyed building was completed in about two months. We also met here a number of professors who had a collaborative project with economics department of Osmania University.

(*vi*) **University of Cologne**

Here I visited the Mathematics Institute and the Computer Centre. I discussed their mathematics curriculum in detail. The standard is the same as that of our M.Sc. but there are three additional features : (*i*) Every student has to do two seminar courses in each of which he has to give a 60-90 minutes talk and participate in discussions on seminar talks given by others, (*ii*) every student has to write a thesis after reading a number of research papers, (*iii*) the student goes deeper in either physics or economics and management or biology. However, a student gets the diploma there at the age of about 26 years while our students do M.Sc. at the age of 21-22 years. The student in Germany can do his Ph.D. thesis after another $1\frac{1}{2}$ to 2 years while our students in general take a longer period. After his Ph.D. a student has to do research for another 6 to 8 years, publish about five good papers, before he can be habilitated and hope to get a parmanent appointment as reader or professor and get the right of independent teaching of university students. Before that, he can only be an assistant in tutorials and problem sessions. There are examinations every semester. Thre is also a tough oral examination for Vordiplom at the end of three years and a final comprehensive written and oral examination at the end of five or six years for the diploma. Only half of the students who join the university mathematics course complete it. The computer centre has a Siemens 4004 system and is a central facility available to all departments.

(*vii*) **University of Heidelberg**

Here we visited the South Asia Institute, the Organic Chemistry Department and the Human Genetics Laboratory. At the South Asia Institute, we met German professors working on Indology, modern Indian History and Hindi and met Indians teaching Urdu, Gujarati, Tamil and Bengali there. Many students were writing their theses on Indian subjects, *e.g.*, one was on the Hindi-Urdu controversy in Uttar Pradesh. In the Chemistry Department, the Head told us about the excellent work being done in some of our good universities in India and at the Human Genetics Laboratory, we saw pictures of some good joint work done by Indians and Germans.

(*viii*) **University of Karlsruhe**

Here we had an interesting discussion with the pro-Rector who had been thrice president of the Rectors Conference and we got an analysis of the recent changes in German Universities. We also met one of our students who was attending a fifteen-month international seminar in Chemistry in that University.

(*ix*) **University of Stuttgart**

We formally visited the University and had discussions at lunch with one of the Professors of chemical engineering who had earlier visited I.I.T. Madras and who told us about the work being done at the computer centre at his University.

3. **VISIT TO OTHER SCIENTIFIC ESTABLISHMENTS**

(*i*) **Max Plank Institute for Radio Astronomy at Effelsberg**

The Radio telescope with 100 meters diameter and paraboloidal in shape is the largest trainable dish type telescope in the world. The one at Jordell Bank in England has a diameter of 75 meters and has an accuracy of 2 cms while this one has an accuracy of 1 mm. This can receive wavelengths from 1 cm to 3 meters. It was constructed recently at a cost of about 7.5 crore rupees and most of it was given by Volkswagen Foundation. The rays received from celestial objects are focussed on a noise-free cooled-to-10° absolute amplifier. It is important that the shape of the disc remains a paraboloid and for this, the design was obtained by iterative methods on a computer. It can be taken to 7° above horizon. Its atomic clock has an accuracy of 10^{-11}, *i.e.*, it loses about 1 second in 10,000 years. Its computer works in binary scale. It studies pulsars, *i.e.*, stars which emit light in bursts and it has discovered organic molecules in intersteller space. 150 persons including 70 scientists are working in this Institute.

(*ii*) **Main Plank Institute for Metals Research at Stuttgart**

This Institute with 320 persons has departments of Metal construction, gages in metals, powder metals, structure of alloys, liquid metals, electrochemistry and corrosion, radiation damage to metals, special metals and purification of metals. It has three special laboratories for radiation damage, dangerous metals and special metals.

(*iii*) **Max Plank Institute for Metal Physics at Stuttgart**

This has about 80 scientists and studies superconducturing theories of dislocation, crystal plasticity and has a large electron microscope for studying impurities in metals.

(*iv*) **Max Plank Institute for Educational Research at Berlin**

This Institute started in 1963 with 4 persons and has now 140 persons with 60 scientists. It studies history and philosophy of education, social aims of education and applies sociology, psychology, economics, etc., in education. The professors choose their own projects for study; one of these is on mathematical pedagogy, another on the preparation of a social science research bibliography; still another on innovation and expansion in education and so on. The Institute has also published studies on the state of German Universities.

(*v*) **Institute of Mathematics and Data Processing at Bonn**

This has departments of pure mathematics, applied mathematics, numerical analysis, automata theory, information science, data processing, training of government officials, solution of administrative problems of government and electronics and has about 350 persons working in it. It has three computers, an IBM 360-50, an IBM 370-165 and a Siemens 4004. It has a number of terminals and display units for training purposes and a television camera to project their display units on the walls. The institution conducts a $2\frac{1}{2}$ years' training programming for mathematical technical programmers (one year mathematics, one year computation, $\frac{1}{2}$ year project), a six months' training programme and short-term intensive courses. It is the main centre for advising government departments on the use of computers. Two of the scientists here are : —an Indian postgraduate of Delhi University who did her Ph.D. in Bonn and her German husband. Within two years, it is intended to connect the computer centre here on a network with centres in London, Paris and Dartsmouth in Germany.

(vi) **IBM centre at Stuttgart**

This centre has terminals at Karlsruhe, Freiberg, etc., evaluates objective-type answers of lakhs of students in T V courses conducted by universities, conducts its own T V training programme in electronic data processing and enables people to find their own aptitudes by means of a dialogue with a computer display unit. We discussed the methods used. It was suggested that one should not develop programmes for special purposes, but should aim at developing general purpose programmes.

4. **Discussions on Education and Science**

We held discussions with representatives of the following organisations connected with education and research in West Germany.

(i) **Permanent Conference of Ministers of Education in Bonn**

Since education is a state subject, the need for coordinating educational activities was felt at an early date and this organisation was created in 1948 with the principle of unanimity accepted. This organisation works in close collaboration with the Federal Ministry of Education in evolving common principles and in educational planning.

(ii) **Federal Ministry of Education in Bonn**

The Federal Government's role in educational planning at all levels has been accepted. It makes suggestions and gives funds for implementing the same.

(iii) **Rectors Conference in Bonn**

All universities, technical and pedagogical institutes are members of this conference. The rectors meet once a month for $1\frac{1}{2}$ days and exchange views on common problems like university autonomy, staff structure, self-administration in university bodies, students' and teachers' participation in university affairs, etc.

(iv) **German Academic Exchange Service**

This organisation is concerned with exchange of students and teachers between German and foreign universities and gives fellowships for the same. It also gives travel grants to German

Professors who have invitations from abroad. It provides professors of German language to other countries. This Service started its work in India in 1954 and during the last 17 years about 680 Indian scientists have visited Germany and about 300 German students have visited India through this Service. It gives now about 40 scholarships for Indian students and arranges study programmes of 10 German students in India every year.

(v) **German Research Association**

Its aim is to promote research in Germany. It is a self-administering organisation. It is not a public authority. Rather it is a non-profit registered body and it provides financial support for research, increases the cooperation between German scientists among themselves and with scientists abroad and it advises state and federal governments in matters of research. It supports scientists and scientific libraries. Its members are the 38 universities (one university nominee with 2 votes and one student nominee with one vote) and scientific organisations like the Max Plank Society. The Association has no research institutes of its own, but can help the universities in establishing institutes of theirs. Its budget last year was about 7.5 crore rupees, of which 51% came from the Federal Government, 41.5% from state governments and 7.5% from Foundations. Research schemes submitted to the Association are referred by some of the 385 referees elected by 30,000 Ph.Ds. with three years' post-doctorate experience in Germany. It gives grants to individuals, groups and universities.

(vi) **Alexander-Von-Humboldt Foundation**

This gives fellowships for young post-doctors below 40 years of age, based on good publications. The fellowships are open to all disciplines and all nationalities, purely on merit. There are no quotas for any country. The selection is made by 70-80 German professors. The scholar must return to his country afterwards. Indians get about 40 scholarships every year.

(vii) **Science Council at Cologne**

In Germany the word "science" includes natural sciences, social sciences and humanities. The Council does no research of its own but was formed in 1957 to advise the federal and state governments on all aspects of education and research. 16 scientists and 6 public men nominated by the Rectors Conference, the German Research Association and Max Plank Society, etc., constitute the Scientific Council while 11 representatives of states and 6 representatives of the Federal Government (but with 11 votes) constitute the Administrative Council. The 39 members with 44 votes constitute the general assembly. It made recommendations in 1960 for university education which had a great influence on the development of German education in the sixties. It has made another set of recommendations for the seventies which it hopes will be realised also by 1985. It has 8 standing committees which work throughout the year. There is great freedom for research in FRG and the Science Council wants to ensure the optimum utilisation of resources. The Governments have also set up a planning commission with its function parallel to one of the functions of the Science Council. The Science Council is a sort of Brains Trust for University education and research in West Germany.

(*viii*) **The Educational Council**

This deals with problems of school education and consists of the representatives of the governments, schools, and pedagogial institutes.

(*ix*) **The Indo-German Society**

This Society coordinates the work of 30 branch societies in Germany. Its budget is about 400,000 rupees out of which 40% is government subsidy and 60% is given by private German industries which have contacts with Indian industry. It arranges for exchange of lecturers, films, cultural delegations and holds exhibitions of art, handicrafts, etc. It also helps Indian students and trainees and encourages contacts between Indian and German industrialists.

(*x*) **Federal Ministry of Economic Development**

The Ministry is responsible for channelising the German aid to developing countries including India. We discussed the aid received by India and the development policy concept of the Federal Republic of Germany for the second development decade.

(xi) **Ministry of Education of Berlin City State**

The Ministry is responsible for the two universities in Berlin, three technical schools for technology, economics and social work (conducting three years courses), and pedagogical institutes, etc., for 40,000 students.

(xii) **Indian students**

We met Indian students and research scholars at Bonn, Heidelberg, Stuttgart, Karlsruhe and Berlin and discussed the problems of equivalence of degrees, comparative standards, examinations, jobs in India, difficulties due to lack of orientation courses in India or due to lack of knowledge of German language, etc.

20

A COMPARATIVE STUDY OF INDIAN AND WEST GERMAN SYSTEMS OF EDUCATION

1. Education in West Germany is free till the highest stage. No tuition fee is charged anywhere. At schools, study materials are also supplied free. At the university about one-fourth of the students get merit-cum-means scholarships sufficient to meet their boarding, lodging and book expenses.

2. Education is available generally for 13 years at school and 6 years at the university. A student starts school at the age of 6 (there is provision for kindergarten education from the age of 3 years), and leaves the secondary school at the age of about 19, the age at which our students, in general, get the B.Sc. degrees. The standard of our B.Sc. is higher than that of their abitur (Secondary Certificate) and that of their diploma is higher than that of our M.Sc. To compete with the German system we should be prepared to provide two-year post-M.Sc. courses at our universities.

3. There are $4\frac{1}{2}$ lakhs students in German Universities as against 35 lakhs in our universities, but if we count only students who are above the age of 19, then the number of the students in our universities will only be about 5 lakhs. We

have also to remember that the West German population is only about 12% of ours.

4. The Germans intend to increase their secondary school population four times and their university population two times in next ten or fifteen years. The University population in U.S.A. and other countries is also very high. From this point, we should not put curbs on expansion of our university educacation, but should try to provide more funds for it and make it more relevant to the needs of our society.

5. The average state expenditure per year per student in Germany is 20,000 to 25,000 rupees. In our country, the average is about Rs. 600 per year and in some universities it is as low as Rs. 200 per year.

6. The student has complete responsibility for his learning. There is no spoon-feeding. He can proceed at his own pace and take as many courses at a time as he can manage. There is increasing emphasis on "learning by research" and "training for life-long learning". The students in general do not receive much guidance from teachers and this causes special hardship to foreign students.

7. According to a recent German definition of research, it is acquisition of knowledge which is new to the person concerned by primarily his own efforts. In this sense, all students and teachers have to be constantly engaged in research.

8. The assessment is mainly internal. Assistants and professors grade their students. There are no examiners from outside except in the case of medicine, law, teaching, etc., where there are examiners appointed by the State also.

9. There is a great emphasis on oral examinations, proseminars, seminars and theses. All these are essentially examinations of individual students.

10. Attendance requirements in lectures (though not in seminars) are generally being given up and a student is welcome to study on his own and appear in the examinations.

11. The students are in general genuinely interested in their studies. Where they are not interested, they can leave their

A Comparative Study

studies in the middle and take up jobs because there is full employment. In fact, West Germany has more than two million workers from outside the country.

12. The physical conditions of study are highly satisfactory. Every teacher has an office of his own where he can study undisturbed. The libraries are large with 10-50 lakhs of books in each. Borrowing, return and reminders about books are being increasingly computerised.

13. There is no university with more than twenty thousand students and it is intended not to exceed the limit of twenty-five thousand students in any case.

14. There are no affiliating universities and there are no affiliated colleges. This means that students have to study in large towns and since hostel accommodation is not enough, students have to live as tenants in private houses. This leads to increase in cost of education, but also leads to higher standards. With increase in number of universities and their location in middle-sized towns and with hostel accommodation for thirty per cent of the students (at present it is for twelve per cent only) the situation may ease somewhat in the future.

15. There are no privately-managed colleges and no separate university services. Every permanent employee of a university is an employee of the state government.

16. Since the Government gives more than 95% of the expenses of a university, the government has a great deal of say in the affairs of the university. All appointments of professors, all regulations regarding examinations and even regulations regarding courses of study have sometimes to be approved by the Mininster of Education of the state. Some universities get block grants, but the budgets of many are parts of the state budget. So far, the professor had to negotiate with the ministers direct about the grants to his department. This state is now changing to some extent.

17. Till a few years ago, the full professors were individually demigods in their institutes or departments and collectively they ran the university. The graduate assistants who did a good deal of supporting teaching and the students had no say

in the university affairs. The revolt by the assistants and the students, though motivated by different motives, has resulted in sharing of power in the universities. In some universities, the professors, assistants, students and non-academic staff have seats in the university bodies in the ratio 3 : 3 : 3 : 1. In others it may be 4 : 2 : 2 : 1, but the trend towards sharing of power is quite clear.

18. While in this process of change, the professors have definitely lost both prestige and power, and the assistants and students have got greater participation in university affairs, the government's powers have not much changed. The university autonomy is still respected, but where finances are concerned, the government has got higher powers.

19. Private persons who get into university bodies in India through management committees, graduate constituencies, government and other nominations, have no counterparts there.

20. The students' 'unrest' in Germany was not primarily motivated by unsatisfactory physical conditions of study and play or by fear of later unemployment or by unsatisfactory examination system or by political ambitions of parties. It was more due to the larger powers of the professors and dissatisfaction of students and assistants with this, to the feeling that universities were becoming ivory towers and professors in their search for specialisation and their own scientific reputations did not care to serve the needs of students and of the society, the feeling that vested interests of professors came in the way of radical reforms of curricula, the feeling that university research and teaching served the purpose of capitalists in keeping the weaker section of the society down and in exploiting the people of the developing countries, the feeling that big industrialists and manufacturers of weapons had developed too much power in the world, the feeling that Vietnam War was a fight against imperialist aggressors, the feeling that progressive sections must capture universities to make them tools for socialism and equality and the feeling that the older generation had bungled and the younger generation must accept its responsibilities in world affairs and so on.

21. The students movement in Germany did not lead to strikes on a large scale (in any case, strikes have no meaning in a system in which the students have the main responsibility for learning), nor to gheraos and physical violence, but led to the conceding of the demand for effective participation by students in university affairs.

22. Having got participation, the students realise that they have to spend a great deal of their time in discussions and meetings at the cost of their studies and the professors and assistants find that they have to spend more time in committees at the cost of research. The democratisation process has its demands on time, but the decisions now take into consideration the interests of all sections of the community and university resources are distributed more equitably.

23. One of the results of this change has been the asking of basic questions like the following : What is the goal of education ? Is it acquisition of knowledge or is it changing the society towards higher goals ? What is the need for various courses ? Why should prospective school teachers be taught as if they were going to be university professors ? What should be goals of social sciences or physical sciences ? Why should students study what professors want to teach and why should not professors teach what students want to learn ?

24. The students have accepted the challenge and are equipping themselves through study groups and other means for suggesting radical changes in the educational system.

25. The most active student leaders are "leftist". However there is a section which feels that students must confine themselves to university matters only.

26. Votings in university bodies working according to the new laws show that some assistants side with professors and some with students so that floating votes determine the decisions.

27. The university top executive authority was the rector elected from among the professors for one year. He could continue as pro-rector and could be re-elected. This often led to difficulties in the more complex administrative situations in today's

universities. The trend is to elect rectors for periods from two to six years or to elect presidents from within or outside the universities or to elect a committee consisting of a rector and pro-rectors. Different models are being experimented within different universities.

28. Higher education is a state subject and as such the Federal Government has no direct constitutional rights in this area unlike India where the constitution provides that coordination and maintenance of standards in higher education is the responsibility of the central government (in pursuance of which the UGC was established). However, in Germany, the Federal Government and the eleven state governments have agreed about the joint responsibilities in matters like planning of education, starting of new universities, etc. Thus the Federal Government gives fifty per cent grant for development of an existing university or for the starting of a new university. A state government cannot easily start a new university without the Federal Government's consent, for in that case it would lose fifty per cent grant which is substantial.

29. The traditional German educational system was excellent for training relatively small number of students, but Germany has also experienced an "explosion" in the number of students. The number of university students increased from 188,000 in 1955 to 369,000 in 1965, to 4,26,000 in 1968 and is expected to reach one million in 1980. To meet this increase, existing universities were strengthened and 13 new universities were established between 1961 and 1969 with an expenditure of 300 crores of rupees for 75,000 seats. In the next ten years thirty more universities have to be established so that by 1980, there may be 70 or more universities in West Germany as against about 100 which we have today.

30. There are at present a number of different types of schools, *viz.*, 13-year schools specialising in classics on modern science, 11-year schools of vocational education and so on and once a student has joined a type of school after his four years of primary education, transfer to another type is very difficult. Thus a student has to decide on his future career at an early age. It is now proposed to have comprehensive schools with

more flexible curricula where students will have to make up their minds about their careers at a much later date, say after 9 or 10 years of school education.

31. At the university level also, there are the normal universities, technical universities, technical academies, colleges of sports and music, teacher-training colleges, etc. It is proposed to have now comprehensive universities with flexible curricula so that various types of institutes of higher education could be under one roof.

32. The German universities have at present only one degree, *viz.*, diploma which a student gets after five to six years of study. Thus there is a "master's" degree in German universities, but no "bachelor's" degree. It is now proposed that students may leave the universities after two to three years of study or after five to six years of study. In the Plan prepared by the Science Council, it is proposed that 15 to 18% of an age group students work for a course of about 3 years and 5 to 6% for the course of 4 to 6 years. The first group would have received about 16 years of education and the second group would have received about 19 years of education.

33. There is a significant percentage of foreign students in German universities. In 1969 there were 423,000 German and 27,000 foreign students. In 1980 the numbers are expected to be about 900,000 and 50,000 respectively.

34. In 1969 the total expenditure on school education was about 3,000 crores of rupees and on university education was 1,200 crores of rupees. The total expenditure was 3·3% of gross national product and 10·8% of total public expenditure.

35. In 1966, FRG had 708 students in universities per 100,000 inhabitants. The corresponding figures for UK, France, Japan, Netherlands, USSR and USA were 646, 1,076, 1,285, 1,310, 1,830 and 3,245 respectively. The figure in India would be about 500, but if we have comparable age groups only, it would come to about 100 only.

36. The Max Plank Society runs about sixty research organisations, parallel to the laboratories of Council of Scientific and Industrial Research or of Defence Research and Deve-

lopment Organisation. However, here the students do only fundamental research. The applied research is done by the laboratories of the big industrial establishments. For middle level industries, the government is now setting up cooperative research organisations.

37. The German Research Association gives large scale funds for research to universities. In some cases these may amount to 75% of the research funds of a university. In our country, CSIR, ICSSR and UGC give funds for research projects but there is no organisation for giving funds for large scale projects in universities.

38. Every student in Germany who passes the abitur (secondary school) has a right to get admission in a university, as far as possible in a university in subject of his choice. However, in some subjects like medicine, the demand is more than the number of seats and the student may have to wait for his turn. The selection may even be made partly on merit and partly by drawing of a lottery. No admission tests are held but centralised admissions are made in all such cases.

39. The standards in German Universities are more or less uniform and the expenditure per head is about more or less the same unlike India where expenditure per head varies and standards are different in affiliating, unitary and central universities. There are however some departments here and there which are well-known because of the professors. However, the salary scales are uniform all over the country.

40. The highest paid professor in a university does not get more than five times the salary of a primary school teacher and in most cases it may be only three times. In our case, in spite of our goal of socialism, the professors may get twenty times as much as a primary school teacher. The primary school teacher in Germany, on an average, can get about Rs. 20,00 p.m.

41. The traditional German system had institutions and seminars, each built with a professor as a nucleus, and the governance was in hands of larger faculties consisting of 60 or 70 professors. In the new structure, there will be depart-

ments or schools of studies. Thus faculties have been broken into smaller units and the institutes have been grouped into bigger units. The new system is more like the Indian or the American systems.

42. The staff structure is also now being rationalised and divided into professors, associate professors, assistant professors, lecturers, graduate assistants, etc. Inbreeding is avoided and an associate professor of one university can become, in general, a professor in another university only.

43. There is a great interest in Sanskrit studies and there are more than forty associate and full professors of Sanskrit in Germany. There are many universities which teach modern Indian languages also.

44. German scientists are quite keen to collaborate on those projects in which India offers special problems, *e.g.*, study of certain genetic consequences of diseases prevalent in India but not in Europe, on sociological or economic problems of a developing economy, on study of Jain and Vedic scriptures, on Indology or even on properties of Ayurvedic medicines. They are also realising that good work is being done in India in modern science and mathematics, but this work is not so well known as it should be. Wherever this is known, they are prepared to collaborate.

45. The average student-teacher ratio today is 9 : 1. It is 4 : 1 in medicine, 6 : 1 in science, 9 : 1 in engineering, 14 : 1 in arts and 25 : 1 in law and economics.

46. The strength of the German industry is due to the following factors, among others :

   (*a*) specialised practical training in vocational schools and technical academics training middle-level personnel,

   (*b*) training in teachnical universities with cooperation of persons from industry and meaningful industrial experience even before joining a technical course,

   (*c*) top level scientific work in laboratories of big industrial houses,

(d) specialised "further education" courses outside the university,

(e) fundamental research in Max Plank Society Institutes,

(f) German education system which produces highly motivated responsible young men.

47. Work on new curriculum development in schools and universities has just begun. Innovations in education like use of T.V., tape-recorders, correspondence courses, open air universities are also in the beginning stages. In fact from 1945-56 the main task of German universities was reconstruction of buildings, in 1956-67 the main task was expansion of existing universities and construction of new ones ; in 1967-71 the universities have been restructuring their self-administering organisation in response to students demands.

48. The need for orientation courses for students going to Germany to explain to them the different systems of education there and the need for the more intensive training in German language in India were constantly emphasized to us by Indian students.

21

A COMPARATIVE STUDY OF INDIAN AND AMERICAN SYSTEMS OF HIGHER EDUCATION

1. USA has about 33% of age group 18-24 in higher education, while India has less than 4%. In USA a student has to study for 4 years beyond 12 years of school for getting the first degree. In India, the students usually get the first degree after 2 (or 3) years of a 12 years programme. The percentage of students who continue in the postgraduate programme is very small. Thus the number of students in the 15th and 16th year of education is relatively only about 1% of the corresponding number in USA.

2. The number of students in higher education has been increasing both in India and USA during the sixties. This number became more than double in USA, but in the same period it became more than 3 times in India. In USA the explosion in numbers has almost tapered off and is likely to remain somewhat steady, but in India according to the present trends, the number of students is likely to go on increasing at an exponential rate. At present USA has 9 million students

in higher education which represents 4·5% of the total population of USA. In India we have 3·5 million students which represents about ·68% of the total population. To reach the USA proportion, we should have had about 50 million students in higher education. Moreover, USA has almost reached zero growth rate in population so that at this rate the population is likely to remain steady, while in India there is still a significant growth rate in population and so we may need about 90 million students in higher education by the end of the century if we have to have comparable enrolment in higher education to what USA has today.

3. American students reached the peak of militancy in 1970 and the militant movement almost died down by 1972. In India also student militancy reached its peak before the Emergency, but all the campuses are quiet now.

4. The reasons for students unrest in USA were the Vietnam war, racial inequalities and the demand for students participation in university management. The Vietnam war is over ; some success has been achieved in racial integration and students have been given representation in university bodies. Thus the causes of students unrest have been removed to a significant extent and as such tranquillity has returned to American campuses. In India the causes of students unrest have been : lack of physical amenities, social inequalities, unfairness in examinations, student participation and interference by political parties. With the limited financial resources and with the explosion of numbers in higher education, it is not possible to provide the necessary amenities including sports grounds. Our social system is in a state of upheaval and in spite of all political slogan shouting, social and economic inequalities have not decreased. The examinations continue to be conducted in the same fashion and the problem of student participation in management has not been discussed seriously.

5. Another problem which has serious dimensions in India is that of educated unemployment which has been steadily increasing over the years, This causes frustration and lack of motivation in education. In USA there is almost full

educated employment and as such there is good motivation for learning.

6. In India the cycle sent till recently was : lack of economic growth, leading to educated unemployment, leading to lack of motivation for studies, leading to lower standards in education, leading to less employable graduates, leading to more educated unemployment, leading to decrease in economic growth. In USA, on the other hand, the cycle was : good economic development, leading to full educated employment, leading to better economic growth. In USA recently some trends have been noticed towards unemployment at higher levels of education and this may create some problems in future. In India, on the other hand, Emergency has led to Discipline and optimism.

7. In India the problem of educated under-employment has also been serious in the sense that highly educated people were being employed to do work which less qualified persons could have done. In USA the problem of educated under-employment has just started with many Ph.D.s having been asked to teach in junior colleges and sometimes even in schools. It is good for schools and junior colleges to get highly qualified people, but it is frustrating and improper utilisation of the research experience of these persons.

8. Since in India the teaching jobs were limited and the number of applications was large, a certain element of political manoeuvring and trade union activity had entered into teaching profession. In USA jobs were always available and a teacher could easily leave one university and get a job in another university. However, due to the educational boom being over, in USA similar problems are now being faced. Trade union activity in the teaching profession is increasing and if the trend continues, we may find political manoeuvring of the same type as in India.

9. In USA there is no direct political interference in educational institutions. The two major political parties believe that they do not need agitational methods and students support for getting into power. In India political parties till recently believed that students support could be one important means of getting into power and therefore each political party tried to support extremist students, demands. A stage had been

reached where political parties were giving not only moral and political support, but also financial support to such students' movements. Each political party was having a students wing. However, after the Emergency, the support has ceased.

10. There is a significant difference between the American and Indian examination systems. In USA, by and large, internal assessment prevails and students are examined by their own teachers. There is perfect trust and the students can discuss their marks and grades with their teachers. In their system, it is unthinkable that anybody except the teacher himself should grade the students. In India, on the other hand, except for less than 1% students under the system in IIT's and agricultural universities, the system that prevails is the external examination system where persons, who have not taught the particular student, examine him. This leads to standard questions in examinations, stereotyped examination papers, rigid syllabi, lack of innovation in teaching. This also breeds mistrust between students and teachers. In fact there is no direct contact between students and teachers because they meet only in the lecture halls. In the USA, on the other hand, discussions of answer books provides an important opportunity for students and teachers to meet and discuss academic problems.

11. In American colleges and universities every teacher has a separate office space where he has his own library, where he can study in peace and where he can call students to discuss the assignments and their difficulties. Usually all teachers are present in their offices for about 9 hours a day for 5 days a week and some even come on Saturdays and Sundays to work there. In India, on the other hand, office space for teaching staff is an exception rather than the rule. Teachers very often come just to deliver their lectures and then go back to their homes. Even when they stay on, they can only waste their time in idle gossip, in overcrowded staff rooms. There are no opportunities or places for individual students and teachers to meet and discuss academic matters.

12. The American system provides incentives for teachers to continue to grow. The slogan so far there was "Publish

or perish". Now with greater competition, the slogan has become "Teach well and publish or perish". Sometimes teachers continue to remain on contract appcintments or on probation for 8—10 years and it is only when they reach the professorial rank that they are given confirmed positions. So far, the teachers did not mind because even if they were fired from one place, they could easily get a job in another place. In fact there were graded institutions. A person fired from a first rate institution could get a job in a second rate institution at the same salary. He did not suffer financial loss, though he got the punishment of serving in an inferior institution. Even the thought of this punishment kept everybody on his toes, and with suitable conditions of work, teachers continued to grow academically and professionally.

13. In India on the other hand, there has been no security of service in some privately managed institutions where a teacher could be fired on completely non-academic considerations. As such teachers there were interested in pleasing the members of the management rather than in growing academically. In other institutions perfect security was provided to the teachers and the probation period was normally one year. A teacher in thesein stitutions was sure of earning his increments irrespective of the quality of the work he did. There was no motivation for doing good work and there was no disincentive for doing inferior work. The result has been that teachers do not grow academically and very often they go on repeating the same notes for as long as 10—20 years. With the stagnant knowledge of the teachers, the educational system is bound to stagnate. This is what has happened in India.

14. The teachers in university departments had, however, one incentive, namely, that of going from lecturer's grade to reader's grade or from reader's grade to professor's grade and for this at least some teachers in university departments continued to grow. On the other hand a similar incentive was not available in affiliated colleges and therefore many times even good teachers there become stagnant.

15. Even in the university departments the number of posts in senior grades is strictly limited and fixed. In a depart-

ment usually there is one professor, 3—4 readers and 20 lecturers. A person has to wait till somebody in the senior grade leaves or retires and when such an eventuality happens, there is a big competition for getting that post. There might be 10 applicants from within the department and 10—20 from outside the department and however fair the committee may be, it can select only one. The rest are frustrated and express their frustration through either going to courts or instigating student indiscipline. The frustration of junior teachers has been one major causes of student indiscipline in our country.

16. In USA, the faculty structure is not conical as in India but is pyramidical in the sense that in a department there can be 7—8 professors, 10—12 associate professors and 12—15 assistant professors and the numbers in each range are not rigidly fixed. Every person has a reasonable chance to go up if he continues to do good quality work and if a person does very good work, even a post in a higher grade can be created for him. This also leads to greater democratic working in the American departments, while in the Indian departments there is a great autocracy in the sense that the head of the department is the supreme boss and so long as he is in office, he wields great authority. There is usually no rotation or election of heads of departments as in the American system. The heads further strengthen their position by appointing their own students in the department so that in many cases there is inbreeding. The head gets the implicit obedience of his colleagues, both because they are sufficiently junior to him and because very often they have obtained their doctorate degrees under his own guidance. This leads to very smooth working of the departments but academically the department can wither away unless the head happens to be really an academic person.

17. The system is harmful from another point of view because the head has so much administrative work to do that he finds little time for research and when he does not find time for research, he discourages others from doing research. On the other hand sometimes to keep up appearances he uses his position to add his name as a co-author to the papers of his

younger colleagues. Many students are registered for research with the head of the department, not because they expect him to guide the research efficiently, but because they expect to get jobs more easily if they work under the guidance of the head.

18. Even in research the aim usuallly is not to do good quality research but to get a job through appearance of doing research. This is one factor which is responsible for deterioration in quality of research in India. In USA, on the other hand, departments heads change quite often and as such senior persons can continue to devote all their time to research. Very often the position of the head of the department in USA goes abegging because no senior person wants to take up the responsibility of the headship and quite often assistant professors have to be appointed as heads of departments. In India, on the other hand, the position of the head of the department is a coveted post since all power and prestige are associated with the headship of the department.

19. Professional academic activity has not grown very significantly in India. Moreover, the professional societies are dominated by senior heads of departments who very often are not active in research. A person gains in prestige automatically by remaining head of a department for a long time, without doing significant research and he receives honours and recognition both from the government and the professional societies, his colleagues and his students. From a senior head of the department, nobody wants to ask the awkward question as to whether the head of the department is still active in his field or has become fossilised. This mutual courtesy does a lot of harm to the educational system. In USA, on the other hand, professional societies are very active. The work of every person continues to be continuously evaluated and every one has to work in research in order to remain academically alive. Many of the professors get research grants from the government and sometimes they get their summer vacation salaries out of these grants. These grants are sanctioned by the subject specialists who evaluate the work done by the person concerned during the previous 3—5 years. Thus a person is not likely to get government grant unless he continues to remain active and this

can mean both financial and academic loss. As such every senior person remains active continuously throughout. This provides a great dynamism to the American educational system.

20. Another reason for lack of creativity by senior persons is the system of external examinations and the membership of external experts in university selection committees in India. Most of the senior persons are busy in evaluating answer books of students of other universities for at least 8 months in a year. During the summer months when the American professors are busy in carrying out research project assignments, the Indian professors are busy in dull and monotonous task of evaluating answer books. The American professors get money for doing research work, while the Indian professors get money for evaluating answer books. It is during this period that a professor can get more time to think about research and it is during this time that our Indian research students get almost completely neglected.

21. Another drawback in our system is that senior people have to travel quite a lot in order to make selections for other universities or to attend meetings of their Boards of Studies. Teachers of the departments are not trusted either to make their curricula or to select their own colleagues. This means a lot of travelling by senior faculty members and a corresponding dislocation in their academic activities. In fact one vice-chancellor remarked recently that he met some of his professors more often at the airport than at the university campus. The problem of the absentee professors is also important in USA but usually there the professors are absent for attending research conferences, symposia and so while teaching suffers there also, research gains in the process. In the Indian system, the absentee professor implies weakening both of teaching and research.

22. It will thus appear that the American system provides for academic ambitions to its teachers while in the Indian system the academic ambitions can be extremely limited. The surplus energy of the teachers finds its outlet in non-academic pursuits which ultimately harms the educational institutions.

23. The problem of national integration is important both in India and in USA. In USA it is the problem of integration of black minority into the national main stream. Usually there are still separate black colleges and the percentage of women students and black students is lower than that of male students and white students respectively, but serious efforts have been made in recent years to provide educational institutions where whites and blacks can study in perfect equality and in this effort, the academic community has played a significant role. It is expected that by 1985 USA would have obtained racial balance and even balance between sexes in higher education.

24. In India we also face similar problems on a much bigger scale. The proportion of minorities and of weaker sections of society is still small relative to their population. Though at government level efforts have been made to have more scheduled caste and scheduled tribe students in higher education, the academic community has not shown any great enthusiasm in this direction. The percentage of teachers from minorities and from the weaker sections of society is still very insignificant. The percentage of women teachers is relatively larger but most of them are still teaching in women's colleges. There is not even consciousness of the magnitude of the problem in our country and efforts have been half-hearted. In fact, it is doubtful whether adequate statistics are available and whether some planning has been done so that we can have a target that at least by 1990, we should have every section of society represented in proportion to its population in higher education. If we go at the present place we may not achieve the targets of national integration in higher education even in 40-50 years time.

25. Another problem which we face is that of regional imbalances. Higher education is still the responsibility of the state governments and different state governments have different financial resources and therefore standards of education can be different in different states. We are fortunate in having a University Grants Commission to maintain and coordinate standards but unfortunately its funds are mainly utilised for financing of central universities so that the funds at its disposal

for supporting 90% of the universities are so small and so thinly spread that it can neither help in maintaining nor in coordinating the standards. Unless the maintenance of central universities is made the responsibility of a separate organisation and unless the UGC is given significant funds for equitable distribution over all the universities, regional imbalances are bound to continue and grow. In fact one of the responsibilities of a UGC should be to see that all universities have similar chances of growth and weaker universities receive larger central funds. This is not happening at present. Now that education has come on the concurrent list in the constitution, it is hoped that the UGC will be able to play a more effective role.

26. USA does not have a central University Grants Commission, but it has professional organisations and accreditation agencies which have done useful work in maintenance and coordination of standards. Though there are regional imbalances, they are not as marked as in India.

27. In India we face another problem and this is that we have to give higher education instruction also in about 15 different languages, while in USA there is only one language throughout the country. Providing facilities in one language is much more economical than providing it in 15 languages. We do not have the resources for producing first rate text books, even in one language, while we have to produce all the books in all the languages at the same time. Our educational system has thus 15 sub-systems, while in USA there is no sub-system at all. The number of books of real post-graduate and higher standards in each of the regional languages is not even 1% of what is available in English language for the American institutions. This poses a serious strain on our resources and is a factor to be taken into account whenever we consider raising of educational standards.

28. In USA the expenditure on higher education per student is 3,400 dollars. In India the corresponding expenditure per student is only about Rs. 600/- per year. Thus our expenditure per student is not even 3% of what it is in USA, and then to expect the same returns from the system is to ask for the impossible. This is precisely what our political leadership is doing and is thus blaming the educational system for its own failures.

29. In India by trial and error we have arrived at the cheapest system of education. In USA, on the other hand, due to growing affluence they have arrived at the costliest system in the world. We represent two extremes—one bred by poverty and the other by affluence.

30. In USA there are more than 2,500 autonomous colleges and universities, each one of which is free to determine its own destiny. In India we have about 100 universities and 3,800 colleges. The colleges cannot determine their own destiny and they have to carry out the orders from the universities to which they are affiliated. There is almost no academic freedom for a college to determine its policy of admission or courses or method of examinations and so the teachers of the college do not feel involved in the educational system. In USA every college teacher feels that he has a distinct responsibility for improving the academic tone and reputation of his college and he can contribute to the development of new and more meaningful courses.

31. The system of affiliation in India also means greater obstacles to innovation and experimentation. No new idea can be tried in 60-100 affiliated colleges of different academic standards and sizes at the same time. Since it is not possible for 60-100 colleges to run at the same pace, the policy is to ask them to stand at the same place and this is roughly what happens when no college is allowed to move forward lest others should lag behind.

32. In India there is a large number of government colleges whose administration is supervised by government and whose academic side is determined by the universities ; there are no such government colleges in USA.

33. In USA about 25% of the faculty members have Ph.D. degrees. In India the corresponding percentage would be about 10. At the post-graduate level about 70—80% teachers have their highest qualifications, the same as that of the classes they are teaching.

34. Both India and USA are dissatisfied with their educational systems. The reasons for this dissatisfaction are of course

completely different. Students are also dissatisfied in both the countries, but for different reasons and to different degrees.

35. Mass higher education has been in operation in USA for a larger period of time and so the system has got accustomed to high enrolments. In India mass higher education is a relatively recent affair and the educational system has not been able to absorb all the shocks of explosion of numbers.

36. Students' interests in different disciplines change very quickly though the trend is similar. Both in India and USA students are going to social sciences, arts, law and commerce, and away from the natural sciences. The reasons again are different. In USA there is already sufficient affluence and they believe that modern science and technology have given them enough and it is the social distribution and utilisation of wealth produced that is more important. In India we are still suffering from shortages of all kinds and science and technology are still desperately needed. However, the trend away from science has come from the fact that we have not been able to absorb all the scientists and engineers we have produced in these years.

37. There is a sudden outburst of interest in environmental studies and the universities in USA have been quick enough to respond to this interest by providing courses in these areas. In India similarly population studies and family planning are very important, but few universities have provided meaningful courses on these subjects. The Indian system is more rigid and takes a longer time to respond to challenges than the American system.

38. In India almost all students are full-time students, while in USA quite a sizeable proportion of students study through correspondence courses and evening colleges. In spite of work for more than ten years, the percentage of students in correspondence courses in India is still less than 1%.

39. In India, there is not much possibility of students earning while learning because part-time jobs are not easily available. In USA many students work during summer months and earn enough money to meet their educational expenses for the rest of the year. Sometimes they work for a year and then

study for 2-3 years with the money so earned. In India the unemployment position is so acute that jobs for short periods are not easily available. This makes our students more dependent on the parents than the American students. This also means that only people from relatively richer sections of society can afford to go in for higher education.

40. In USA higher education is the result of affluence, while in India it is the result of a desire for gaining social status and moving upwards in society. Since it is a status symbol, efforts are made to acquire the status symbol at any cost. Knowledge for its own sake is not a strong motivating force here.

41. For students who face prospects of unemployment in later life, the lure of a political career is very attractive. Students with some capacity for organisation and rhetoric are thus attracted to try to use the student's platform for making a future political career. They do not mind using their fellow students as guineapigs. Moreover, due to social conditions in society, they have enough causes to exploit for their own purposes. They can give the feeling to the students that fighting social injustice is much more important than getting education. In USA there are thousands of other careers which are open to bright students and as such the political career does not have the same attraction and no student tries to use his position as an elected representative to climb on the political ladder. Fortunately the Emergency has removed this attraction from the Indian education system also.

42. In India many students do not expect much from the universities except shelter from the difficult conditions of life outside the universities and a degree at the end of their stay as a possible passport to higher studies. Universities also do not expect much more from them and standards are sufficiently diluted to meet the needs of the less-motivated students. In fact, students feel the need for shelter so much that many of them like to stay as long as possible in the colleges and universities, specially because education is a highly subsidised activity.

43. The threat to university autonomy in India comes not only from governments which are anxious to use educational institutions for remaining in power or from political parties

which want to use universities for getting centres of influence; it also comes from pressure groups of students, teachers, karamcharis, etc., who may be interested in exploiting the economic resources for higher education as much as possible. In USA, these other threats are almost absent.

44. The administrative structure at the top level in Indian universities is quite weak. Usually there are no officers corresponding to vice-presidents and administrative deans in American universities. A vice-chancellor has to control single-handed all the facets of university life, while in USA the president can rely on many senior persons for administrative help. In India when the vice-chancellor asks for administrative help from his academic faculty, he has a guilty conscience because these persons can do administrative work only at the cost of their academic work, but he cannot help it because he does need help at that level and the government is not prepared to provide senior full-time administrative help.

45. Higher education in India is further weakened by the moral weakness in the political and social structure. The atmosphere of mistrust and of corruption and nepotism makes innovations in higher education extremely difficult. It is becoming extremely difficult to reform the examination system, not because we do not know the remedies, but because real remedies have to ultimately depend upon the character of the people operating the system. If there is no mutual trust, the system cannot easily work.

46. Universities in India completely depend on state financial help. Very few universities in India have any significant endowment and they cannot carry out any innovation without convincing the government authorities since all innovations do require some financial commitment. In some universities, even a vice-chancellor cannot create the post of a peon without the sanction of the state government. It must, however, be said that in quite a number of universities financial powers given to the universities were misused in the interest of some groups of teachers and others with the result that the state governments felt obliged to step in. Universities have in general not shown sufficient internal strength to resist external

Study of Indian & American System

pressures. In USA, on the other hand, there are quite a number of universities, where significant income comes from private endowment ; this gives some desirable flexibility and independence to the American educational system.

47. There is much less innovation and experimentation in India than in USA. The reasons are both finanical and social. Innovation and experimentation cost money, require hard thinking, courage to implement new ideas and a backing from a society encouraging all new ideas. Moreover, Indian higher education is today fighting for survival and when survival becomes a dominant value, development considerations are relegated to the background. In USA survival is taken for granted and development has to be worked for.

48. Our Indian educational system produces students of the highest calibre, but the average quality of students it produces is quite low. Our best students who have gone abroad can compete with the best in the world, but our average is nowhere near the average of the developed countries. When we talk of raising our educational standards, we have to keep in mind the average students.

49. In India, all attempts at improvement of higher education have been centrally directed and due to the diversity of conditions and the large size of the country, they have not succeeded. In USA, on the other hand, every university has tried to develop according to its own genius. As such the attempts at improvement have been decentralised and have succeeded.

50. The progress of book production in regional language has been very slow, while regional languages are being increasingly used as media of instruction. As such the standards of education have suffered. In USA text books are being produced on a large scale since there is only one language in the country and there is a big market for books. Moreover, students can afford to buy good books, but in India most of the students have to depend on cheap books only.

51. In USA students evaluation of teachers is prevalent on a large scale. A large number of courses are evaluated by the

students and evaluation is used by the teachers in improving their teaching. In India students are not being asked to give their opinions even anonymously or confidentially about the courses given by the various teachers. In fact some students want attendance to be made optional so that students can express their disapproval of teaching by some teachers by being absent from their classes. Again, whenever there is a talk of student evaluation, it is discouraged because it is argued that interested parties can always get adverse or favourable reports from the students. This again shows how mistrust harms the system.

52. Though no effective survey has been made in Indian universities, it appears that the average time an Indian student spends in studies per week may be about 50% or less as compared to the American student. No system can produce good results unless it can motivate the student to put in hard work.

53. Professional activity in India in the field of higher education is limited to teachers' organisations which lay a great deal of emphasis on service conditions of teachers. There is no organisation for higher education research and development which represents all elements in higher education, namely, educational administrators in colleges, universities and government organisations, teachers at all levels and persons interested in higher education from other walks of life. Such an organisation can play a very healthy role in the development of higher education in India.

22

INNOVATIVE IDEAS AND PRACTICES IN HIGHER EDUCATION

1. *Carnegie Commission On Higher Education* has called for less time and more options in education beyond the high school and a major overhaul of the nation's (American) higher educational system. Included in its recommendations are : a three-year bachelor's degree programme, university accreditation of high schools to offer the equivalent of a first year of college, offering of some degree after every two years of study, wide use of two new degrees, *vtz.*, the Doctor of Arts and the Master of Philosophy, reduction by one or two years of time required to earn a Ph.D., availability of college-study alternatives, such as apprenticeship and military programmes and expansion of educational opportunity for women, older people, workers and the poor.

2. *Carnegie Commission Report of 1971* encourages three-year undergraduate programmes offering students more options:

    (*a*) in lieu of formal college,
    (*b*) to defer college attendance,
    (*c*) to step out from college in order to get service and work experience, and

(d) to change direction while in college ; to promote lifelong education ; to simplify degree structures ; and to reduce the emphasis on formal certification.

3. *Chicago State College and North-Eastern Illinois State College* are members of a 20-college consortium *"University Without Walls"* programme under a $415,000 grant from the Dept. of Health, Education and Welfare. There are no degree requirements, no prescribed time for getting a degree and unlimited opportunities to learn outside the classroom and campus. Each student designs his own individualized programme, with guidance of a faculty adviser based on his own interests. The programme is based on two central principles ; that relevant learning can take place in many locations, in the classroom, on the job, in individual work projects and in the give and take of seminar discussions, and that a variety of geographical locations can broaden a student's horizons and help him gain perspectives that are not possible within the confines of a single campus.

4. *University Without Walls (UWW)* is a network of varied alternatives on different campuses which emerged from a proposal of some 100 professors attending *Project Changeover* in the summers of 1967-69. Out of these sessions emerged the plan for the University Without Walls designed and fostered by the *Union for Experimenting Colleges and Universities*, financed by grants from the U.S. Office of Education and the Ford Foundation. The UWW expands the range of activities that may help students learn through a *director of learning resources*, on and off-campus, for an age group of 16 through 73 taught by academicians, professionals, and non-professionals. A related programme operating on the same basic principles as the UWW is the *Union Graduate School*, which is also sponsored by the Union for Experimenting Colleges and Universities. This is keyed to the postgraduate student working under his own direction towards a doctorate. These are selected students with high potential and a demonstrated ability to direct their own study. Unresolved problems (and opportunities) of the UWW include its breadth of constituencies, its individually adapted programmes, its wide range of learning resources and its diverse adjunct faculty.

5. *The 1972 report of the University Without Walls programme states* : "Some 3,000 students in age group 16-73 from various back-grounds are now enrolled. A number of units have an un-usually high proportion of Blacks and Puerto Ricans. The structures of each unit of UWW has been devised by a team of students, faculty and administrators. The units have been concerned more with student motivation and life achievements than with test scores or academic grades. Each student follows a programme tailor-made by the student and his adviser who is considered a learning-facilitator. Students use a variety of learning experiences to achieve their objectives : regular course work, internship, apprenticeship and field experiences; independent study and individual and group projects; travel, programmed material, cassettes and other technological materials. There is no prescribed curriculum or a uniform time schedule for completing the degree. Students study in variable time-frames. Graduation takes place when the student has achieved the learning objectives agreed upon with his adviser, be it in four or ten or twenty years after he begins.

Most students work with one or more *adjunct professors*, men and women in business, social services, government, scientific research, artistic creativity and other occupations, who are giving time to help under-graduates acquire related competence. *An Inventoy of Learning Resources* developed at each institution guides students and advisers in planning the student's educational experiences."

6. *Board of Regents, University of the State of New York* (not to be confused with the State University of New York) has established 'Regents External Degrees' (Associate in Arts, and Bachelor of Science in Business Administration). The A.A.'s estimated cost is approximately $ 150 in fees and that of B.S. is about $ 400. These require no formal or informal instruction. Candidates must pass proficiency examinations demonstrating that in some way (practical experience, independent study, etc.) they have acquired the equivalent of a college education.

7. *Regents of The University of the State of New York (1970)* state : "Students entering school today will spend more than half their lives in the next century. While predictions of

what the world will be like in the twenty-first century must be inexact, two conditions seem certain; improvements in communications and in travel, and growth in international trade will multiply the contact between people and nations; and a range of economic, health, and political problems resulting from increasing population will remain unsolved and will create social unrest....What kind of education is needed for such a world as this one promises to be in the twenty-first century? The *Commission on International Understanding* in 1964 declared firmly for an education that transcends differences of country, race and political allegiance.

"If future generations of Americans are to acquire competence for living in the world of tomorrow, their education must transcend its customary limitation to the ways of life and patterns of thought that characterize Western civilization....A man must come to see himself in relation to his total environment in space and time, and so to locate himself on the map of human experience. This entails both the analysis of similarities and the perception of differences, both an understanding of the cultural tradition that has helped to shape him, and a knowledge of competing traditions which provide a standard of comparison. ..."

8. *The Empire State Callege* of the State University of New York, established in 1971, has no campus of its own, offers an associate of arts and bachelor's degrees to high school graduates of any age on a first-come first-served basis. The college has established learning centres throughout the state so that state residents will be within commuting distance of a centre. Each centre is to serve about 400 students. On admission, the student joins an orientation workshop where he shares his interests and tentative plans with faculty members and other students. After this, the student makes an appointment with a *Mentor* and together they design a plan of study which can be either full-time or half-time depending upon the student's other commitments and upon the amount of time and energy he is prepared to invest. This plan becomes then a *Learning Contract*. When the contract is over, the student plans another sequence of work with the same mentor or some other.

The College offers three basic modes of learning. In the *Discipline mode*, a student pursues a particular body of knowledge. In the *Problem mode*, a student concentrates on a major social issue or a comprehensive unit of study which draws upon diverse kinds of skills and knowledge. In the *Experience mode*, a student uses on-the-job experiences or other activities which enlarge his understanding of experiences and improves his capacity to function effectively in them. Many different kinds of situations, materials and activities may be employed: museums, libraries, schools, industries, social welfare organisations, cultural events, correspondence courses, T.V., CAI, evening classes, travel and study in other states or abroad.

The College works on four assumptions. First, that a student's needs and purposes are an effective starting point for learning and programme development. Second, that effective learning combines thought and action : combines direct experiences with reading, writing and reflection. Third, that learning can be pursued in diverse places, at several times and in several ways. Fourth, that individual students differ in the processes of learning they can usefully employ as well as in the competence and awareness they need to develop.

9. *The Newman Report on Higher Education.* 1971 sought reconstitution of colleges and universities for persons of all ages. The advantages claimed are that entering students would have experiences outside formal education which would strengthen their motivation and increase their ability to choose 'relevant' courses; entering and learning according to individual need would become socially legitimate and involuntary attendance would be discouraged; costs would be lower because students and institutions would be more effective.

The report further recommended (*a*) admission policies should favour students with experience from outside school, (*b*) discrimination against part-time students should end, (*c*) subsidies should be developed to aid "second chance" opportunities through pension funds, social security system, education banks, etc., (*d*) internship, cooperative education programmes and work-study programme should be expanded, (*e*) new regional examining universities should be created to give examinations, credits and degrees, (*f*) regional television colleges and tape libraries should be established, (*g*) learning clinics owned and operated by faculty members should be permitted, (*h*) new curricula for minority and women institutions should be developed.

10. At *"Experimental College"* at S an Francisco State College, the central ideas are : Students ought to take responsibility for their own education, learning starts but never ends, takes place everywhere anytime, with anything; self-directed learner is both the in-put and out-put.

11. *Independent Experimental Growth Programme* with a multi-discipline battery of tests and interviews discusses plans, interests, problems, needs, strengths, weaknesses with each student. When this information is fed into the computer, it presents for him printout of alternative courses, with various sequences; faculty members with most adaptable teaching style to his learning style; books, references, annotated bibliographies; students, faculty, resource-persons on and off campus with similar interests and concerns; work-study and travel opportunities geared to his abilities and needs and alternative ways to learn.

12. *City College of New York* has instituted a new off-campus degree programme which allows students to share in planning up to one-quarter of their credits in other than classroom work. With a faculty panel they will choose the off-campus activities which consist of employment, voluntary service or travel.

13. *The Carnegie Corporation* in 1971 recommended strong development of non-traditional study whose purpose is to use all types of off-campus study, credit by examination and external degree programmes. The report suggested a number of reasons for the growth of non-traditional degree programmes : (*a*) need to reach new kinds of people not traditionally served by higher education, (*b*) need for flexibility, options and imaginative experimentation in higher education, (*c*) earlier maturity of young students and their desire for more indepen-

Innovative Ideas and Practices in Higher Education

dence and initiative, (*d*) recognition that learning is a life-long process and is not something to be confined to a fixed age or to prescribed academic setting, (*e*) the fact that more education takes place before college, outside college and after college than ever before, (*f*) growth and refinement of T.V., taped casettes records and computers as learning aids for individualised self-directed study and (*g*) reduction in cost.

14. *Brockport State College, State University of New York* has inaugurated an off-campus degree programme whereby a student can earn a bachelor's degree in liberal arts (requiring no foreign language). They may study in campus and extension courses inside and outside the state system and through educational T.V. and correspondence courses.

15. *School of Education, University of Wisconsin* has devised a system of one-credit five-week training modules to replace the more rigid requirements of the conventional teacher education curriculum. The school has adopted a decentralized system of mini-courses which the student may assemble to suit himself.

16. *State University of New York and New York State Education Department* with a grant of $ 1·8 million from the Ford Foundation have initiated a two-year off-campus college degree programme. SUNY will establish a non-residential undergraduate college in which students, under faculty direction, will pursue individual programmes through correspondence work, television, counselling and occasional seminars at one or more of the University's seventy campuses. The State Education Department will award an associate or bachelor's degree to persons who pass the required number of college level examinations, regardless of the manner in which they prepare for these examinations.

17. *Skidmore College Troy, N.Y.* has developed an external degree-type programme which would allow persons 16 to 60 to participate. The programme calls for (*a*) abandoning prescribed curriculum, grades and credit points, (*b*) enlarging the faculty to include people outside the college, (*c*) using new techniques for communication of knowledge and (*d*) placing emphasis on the student's self-direction in learning.

18. *Chicago City College of The Air* in 15 years has offered a Junior College programme exclusively over T.V. The college has awarded more than 100 degrees for work completed entirely by T.V., including many handicapped persons and some prison inmates.

19. *American Association of Colleges for Teacher Education* has recommended: changing the curricula to reflect the societal needs and realities with which schools should be formed; balancing the role of education between the citadels of rational thought and the agency of social change.

20. *Ford Foundation* has awarded grants to two university centers which have experimented with ways of counteracting the alienation of students by engaging their feelings and attitudes in the learningpr ocess. The Laboratory of Confluent Education, University of California at Santa Barbara and the Centre for Humanistic Education, University of Missouri, Amherst, will use the grants to develop "humanistic" or "affective" curriculum and teaching methods at all levels from elementary to university, awarding master's and doctoral degrees and at the same time cooperate with university programmes in teacher education, student guidance and school administration.

21. *University of Hawaii* has developed new, inexpensive, long-distance educational exchange by radio, uses artificial earth satellite to convey information instantaneously by voice, print and picture between classrooms, laboratories and libraries in different countries. University of Hawaii will be the main ground station in a network eventually encompassing colleges, universities and other service agencies throughout Pacific and Asia. Scholarship students from Asia en route to Hawaii by sea receive their college orientation beamed to them while they are thousands of miles away. Range of the satellite reaches from Japan to Chile, roughly one-third of the world.

22. *United States Office of Education* is exploring new approaches which would :

    (*a*) promote greater access to post-secondary education for all ages and ability groups,

(b) promote variable time lengths for students to gain degrees,
(c) allow for freer exchange of students between institutions,
(d) make possible interesting combinations of work and study programmes,
(e) demonstrate the advantages of new technologies in teaching,
(f) substitute experience/self-education for course requirements.

23. *University of Pittsburgh* (school of education) gives course on the "Open Classroom" which permits students to follow their own inclinations and interests in classroom study.

24. *Hampshire College*, Amherst, Mass., expects its students to wrestle most with questions of the human condition. What does it mean to be human ? How can man become more human ? What are human beings for ? One sees such questions being personal and yet global. They can be illuminated by historical study, the social sciences, the natural sciences, literature, the lively arts, philosophy and language. They need to be approached with the discipline of intellect, the drama of feeling, the demanding kinesthetic of action, they lead into far fields and abstract knowledge; equally they lead into the immediate contact with daily life, with its joys and terrors, its obligations and rewards, its emptiness and fullness. They demand ultimately the paradoxical combination of detachment and commitment that only the educated can have.

25. *The College for Human Services*, New York has a curriculum on learning to serve the community and many social service organisations provide part-time faculty members for its programmes.

26. *In Sweden* the Ministry of Education is promoting a state-financed "school for life" which students may enter and leave on a continuing basis throughout their lifetime.

27. *The Agency for Cultural and Technical Cooperation* has created an "International School" in Bordeaux,

France, with two centres—one for "training in modern administrative techniques" and the other for "an introduction to present life in the Third World".

28. *Japan's open University*, called the "University of the Air" (radio) gives 4 days a week programmes in domestic science, literature, industrial administration and engineering with courses to be added. Estimated time for earning a degree from the university is four years; no entrance examination is required so as to ensure that the university truly "educates the people". More than 110,000 people are now taking college courses by correspondence.

29. In Australia instead of an open-type university, a *National Resources and Accrediting Institution (NRAI)* has been proposed to provide a 'second chance' to those who have missed out on tertiary education and to reduce social injustice. The NRAI would work with and through existing institutions and would seek to smoothen transfer between them. Its functions would be :

   (*a*) to provide academic programmes for use by universities and colleges of advanced education for both external and internal students,

   (*b*) to create a library of high quality programmes produced by existing institutions and administer their distribution,

   (*c*) to construct, print and distribute 'learning packages' including assignments, tests and examinations for the courses,

   (*d*) to make and distribute tutorial guides for courses.

30. *The permanent staff of NRAI* would consists of educational technologists, producers, editors, academic programme supervisers, academic administrative officers and administrative staff. It would also have staff seconded from other institutions for periods of six months to three years to form course production teams with permanent staff. The NRAI would also have part-time counsellors and tutors from the existing tertiary institutions. Regional centres would normally be situated in existing tertiary institutions and would be used by existing students when internal students put less pressure on facilities.

31. The large-scale use of *Educational Technology* has been tried in many universities in different permutations and combinations :
   (a) replacement of lecture courses by a combination of 'tutorless tutes' and seminars,
   (b) use of carrel programmes incorporating programmed instruction, single concept films and audio-tapes,
   (c) experimental use of computer aided instruction,
   (d) replacement of cook-book practical class instruction by 'open-ended' laboratory experiments,
   (e) replacement of conventional laboratory experiments by computer-simulated experiments,
   (f) use of a library of learning resources containing films, cassettes, books, video tapes, etc., to be used by the student at a time convenient to him in a sequence suggested to him through the use of media themselves,
   (g) use of tape-recorded lessons in conjunction with a text-book. The student reads the text-book with his eyes and hears in an earphone detailed page-by-page explanation of the basic ideas contained in the book,
   (h) use of closed-circuit TV for teaching students on a campus.

32. Programmes in which the *entire responsibility for learning is given to the student* have been tried in some institutions. The faculty members remain available in their offices. A student can consult them whenever he likes and whenever he considers himself ready for a course, he can request for an examination. For each course he is subjected to a three-hour gruelling oral test and declared qualified or not. There are no lectures except tape-recorded ones and there are no laboratory demonstration experiments except those on films. However, all learning aids are made available.

33. We deplore the educational processes that dehumanize... where the organized system, its role playing, its competitiveness, its canned culture, its public relations and its avoidance of risk and self-exposure, its deadly sublimination, all force us all to kill the genius in each of us. *Harry Linogrew*

34. We have to give all undergraduates some sense of the larger world community and to show them the great forces at work in the world.
W. Marvel

35. We see a relationship between higher education as a service industry whose product gets distributed in a system at least analogous to a market system. The market is the one in which the student buys educational status *via* credit hours and grade points, and pays for it with money and by attending classes and doing what he is told to do, which is to read books his teacher finds interesting and remember somethings his teacher considers important, and perhaps think creatively and intelligently about these things. Teachers however tend to think of themselves as dispensers of knowledge, not status, and often resent the attention students pay to credit and grades.

Shellenberg

36. Our main task must be not to provide more facts but an atmosphere where students learn how to learn; where they come to understand that they must continue learning all their lives and where they develop the habits and attitudes to successfully do this. The most effective way of achieving this end is to provide them with surroundings where knowledge is changing; to expose them to the kinds of minds and men which are changing our world.
Clinton Crook

37. New college programmes reflect a variety of new directions; increased emphasis on independent study; greater use of field and off campus experiences; emphasis on general education; use of freshman seminars, tutorials, and other small-group approaches to certain subject-matter areas; reducing of the number of courses a student takes at any one time; increased use of learning aids such as films, tape recordings and other audio-visual devices; cooperative use of facilities; and use of summer sessions and special winter terms to enrich as well as accelerate the student's educational experience. Students at the first year's college level may be more ready to accept and accomplish independent study than the more mature upper class students. There is a greater readiness on the part of the younger students to accept the newer teaching methods, partly because they have not been 'contaminated' on the college level

by an additional two or three years of teacher-directed learning, and partly because college is supposed to be different.

Sam Baskin

38. There are 10 directions for educational change :
    (a) At all levels of education, from pre-school through the university, there is a need to move from a mass approach to teaching and learning to a highly individualized approach.
    (b) Less emphasis on cognitive learning is called for. New ways are needed to develop aesthetic sensory and emotional characteristics.
    (c) The school should not be like a castle surrounded by a moat to protect it from influences of the outside community. It should be an institution in aid of the community it serves.
    (d) Technology must be harnessed for educational purposes, not viewed as a threat.
    (e) A move from a negative to a positive attitude towards children who are "different" is needed, from pre-school nurseries through graduate schools.
    (f) A need exists to develop a multi-cultural curriculum and experience for all young people.
    (g) There should be a review of the credentialing system to give greater importance to performance and behaviour as criteria for determining competency.
    (h) Revision of the "packing order" to recognize the worth of vocational and technical subjects is necessary.
    (i) The climate and environment of educational institutions, now often bleak and inhibiting, should be made free and stimulating for faculty and students.
    (j) The time has come to plan a decent funeral for the faltering concept of the self-contained teacher in the self-contained classroom. The instructional team is now essential, as are differentiated, flexible ways to organize and utilize time and talent.

Don Davies

39. The goal of education is not to increase the amount of knowledge but to create possibilities to discover, to create men who are capable of doing new things.

J. Piaget

40. The nature of college communities at present is based on the assumptions of divisions of scholarship, authority and mission, often competing rather than complementing each other. University education is the strategic factor in the life of each individual community, nation and the world, yet we are in conflict about educational means and ends. How can societal influences such as urbanization, automation, population mobility, racial autonomy, socio-economic differentials, ecological deformities, national and international tensions, often life itself be made more livable and certain ? How can education better prepare one to think and act in terms of the social dimensions, relations and systems designed to modify ethnocentrism that emotional and provincial outlook which assumes the inherent superiority of one's racial cultural group and shows ignorance or contempt for the ways of others ?

41. Considering the fads, fashions, fancies, fables and fallacies in higher education, we find that education has been one of the prime stimuli in our society, but has proved to be one of the areas with a strong resistance to the use of technology for its own purposes......the prevailing annual calendar of higher education is agrarian based in an era of urbanism, space travel, and diminution of farm production...everything is fair game for study on a college campus except higher education itself...one can and may frequently do have a bachelor and master of science of education degree and no credits in education. One can have a doctor of philosophy degree without ever having taken a course in philosophy...most centers of higher education which are designed to free mankind from ignorance, seldom, if ever, have any significant salutary impact on the problems, the people, and the progress of the geographical areas in which they are located.

Beeler and Eberlee

42. "Less teaching and more learning" has been a goal of enlightened educators since Comenius pleaded for it in the 17th

century. The communication scholar McLuhan calls for such change. "The young in many countries continue daily to manifest revulsion against the traditional effort to contain the educational processes in the bureaucratic and homogenized spaces of existing schools and colleges and curricula". A 1969 poll, conducted for Life magazine by Louis Harris Associates, showed a large majority of both high school students and their teachers eager for innovation. Both groups wanted more field work outside the school and more opportunities to work directly in the community. Georg B. Leonard foresees academic courses that would enhance, through seemingly extraneous material, the central nervous system's capacity to make connections which are not necessarily conceptual, factual or symbolic.

43. The scheme of evaluating intellectual attainment by the course with credit method assumes that having taken and passed a course is evidence that a certain body of knowledge is possessed and that not having taken this course is evidence that this body of knowledge is not possessed. Neither of these assumptions are true. There is growing recognition of the need for integrating the knowledge that our students acquire. We refuse to realize that the course-credit system prevents the integration we are seeking. The system emphasizes formal teaching and not learning. It puts the free-ranging intellect into a strait-jacket and is one of the worst possible ways of inducing a person into the life of the intellect.

Nutting

44. All the evidence that I have been able to collect indicates that if there were not a single student added to the present enrolment of American colleges and universities during the next ten years, we would have exactly the same need for scrapping our present system of instruction and inventing a new one—what we have now is a highly mechancial system for disseminating information. Once the information is conveyed, it is checked and academic credits are awarded for accuracy in recording...The present system is built on the assumption that learning occurs in one dimension, the dimension of memory. It assumes that the rewards of learning are not to be found in the pleasure and joy of the knowing or in the achievement of

belief, not in finding a sense of personal and intellectual identity but in receiving credit, social status, a higher income and an exemption for the necessity of further study or intellectual development....The present system of lectures, text-books, survey courses, standard requirements of subject-matter, examinations, and numerical grades...fails to touch the inner consciousness of the student or to deal with his motivation, his emotions, his aims and his needs.

Harold Taylor

45. Those who have knowledge have a peculiar responsibility to be sensitive to the ills of the world, for if they are not, then it will be the ignorant who will be the movers of events, and the value of knowledge will be lost.

Kenneth Boulding

46. A great weakness of traditional education in the Western world is that it is looked upon largely as a process of transmitting a body of received knowledge, information, and conventional skills, from one generation to the next and too little as a process of creating sets of attitudes and talents conducive to finding new and more effective ways of doing thing.

H. Millikan

47. There is a need to make higher education intrinsically more significant. Higher education has served effectively as a screening device for the higher professions, although its imperfection in this regard is evidence by the continuing high drop-out rate of qualified students in good academic standing. It is true that college graduates earn more money in their lifetime than nongraduates do. Yet with respect to the important matters of values, beliefs, and standards of personal conduct, collegiate education has not had a substantial impact on the lives of students.

Mayhew

48. The most rapidly growing segment of American education is the "education periphery", a term used by Moses (1970) to describe systematic educational activities which go on outside the educational core of elementary, secondary, and higher education. Included in the periphery are :

(a) Programmes sponsored by employers—business, government and industry,

(b) proprietary schools, usually run for profit and including beauty schools, computer training, refrigeration schools, etc.,
(c) antipoverty programmes such as the Job Corps and Manpower Training and Development Centers,
(d) correspondence courses,
(e) educational television which is beginning to perform educational functions for all ages—from sesame street to sunrise semester and
(f) adult education programmes ranging from academically oriented evening courses to neighbourhood social action groups concerned with affective learning.

In 1970, 64 million people in USA were pursuing structured educational activities in the education core, whereas about 60 million were in the periphery. By 1976, the number in the core will be approximately 67 million, compared to 82 million in the rapidly growing periphery. Thus with little or no attention from the educational establishment, millions of citizens are creating their own lifelong learning models of education outside the confines of the traditional educational system. Why are we so tied to the credit-hour system despite the overwhelming evidence that it has little value as a measure of education and worse yet stands as a deterrent to flexible programmes of education ? Why despite all the very practical, obvious applicated research on advanced placement, do we still have colleges requiring all freshmen to start at the college's starting point rather than at the students ? Why are we so addicted to the class lecture despite research showing equally good, and frequently better, alternatives ? There seems to be no escape from the conclusion that we do not educate as well as we know.

49. *International University of the World* idea was strongly supported as it was believed that students may study in various cooperating universities of the world and get their degrees from

IVOW. Even now there are cooperative programmes where students can study in different parts of the world and if charter flights are used and cheap dormitories are used, the costs would not be high. UGC may encourage some Indian universities to undertake such cooperative programmes.

50. *The United Nations University* is a new type of institution of higher learning. It will not give degrees but would stimulate thinking and research in subjects llke international relations and peace, problem of peace keeping, arms control and disarmament, human rights, international communication, international problems of development, population and youth, problems of environment and of impact of science and technology on it. The university has also to anticipate problems likely to become of major international and regional concerns and to promote research in order to obtain practical results.

The U.N. University will provide new opportunities for fruitful contacts between scholars of developing and developed countries in investigating problems of reducing economic, scientific and technological gaps between these countries.